NATURE'S BOUNTY FOR YOUR TABLE

Dr. Duane R. Lund

A HOW TO DO IT BOOK
with scores of recipes

Distributed By
Adventure Publications
P.O. Box 269
Cambridge, MN 55008

Copyright © 1982 by
Dr. Duane R. Lund
Staples, Minnesota 56479

Printed in the United States of America

1st Printing 1982
2nd Printing 1989

ISBN 0-934860-20-3

Table of Contents

CHAPTER V MORE FROM YOUR FISH

CHAPTER VI PRESERVING MEATS

CHAPTER VII THE WILDERNESS AS YOUR GARDEN

Introduction

For more years than not, mankind living on this part of the continent was totally dependent on nature for survival. It is likely that only five percent of human history here is "white history". Archaeologists tell us that farming was unknown to the region until about 1000 AD when the Dakota Sioux brought agriculture to the plains areas of the Upper Midwest, growing such crops as maize, squash and pumpkins. It may be that farming was not introduced to the Indians living in the Woodlands until the coming of the famous French explorer, Pierre La Vérendrye, to the Lake of the Woods in 1732. For several thousands of years before that, man accepted Nature's bounty just as she offered it.

The wilderness was good to early man:
- It gave him food in the form of game, fish, wild rice, berries, nuts, wild vegetables and maple sugar;
- The bark of certain trees and the hides of larger animals provided shelter as the walls for his pole-frame dwelling, and even made transportation easier by making a water-proof covering for his canoe;
- Skins and furs made comfortable clothing;
- Plants and herbs were used as medicine;
- Utensils were made of hardened clay;
- The projectile heads of weapons were chiseled from rock; and
- Wooden-shafted arrows were guided to their marks by feathers and propelled by bows of ash or maple drawn taut by a string made from such exotic materials as the sinews of the snapping turtle.

All of which testifies to the bounty of Nature and the creativity of early man.

Mother Earth still provides the natural resources from which we now fashion everything from automobile parts to computers, but if we were suddenly deprived of the fruits of our technical "know-how", could we still survive on what Nature directly provides as did the first men in this area? Yes—individuals no doubt could—but there is not enough to provide for the relatively huge population of today. However, as we have become more and more dependent on our sophisticated manufacturing and marketing systems, we have come to ignore much of what nature still has to offer free for the taking without complicated processing. In fact, a good deal of quality food is simply going to waste.

In this day of energy shortages, high prices and contaminated foods, once again more and more people are looking to nature for their needs. To the surprise of many, the food they bring to their table often has more flavor and is more satisfying than that purchased in the market. And as they harvest Nature's bounty, they have the added pleasure of spending more time in the out-of-doors.

So if you are interested in—
- quality, uncontaminated foods,
- new taste delights,
- saving dollars from your marketing budget, and
- having a good excuse to spend more time out-of-doors. . .

READ ON!

chapter I

MAPLE SYRUP AND SUGAR

The Indians of the Upper Midwest and Ontario cherished maple products. Sugar was preferred to syrup because it could be more easily stored and transported. When added to water it made a tasty beverage and was used as a flavoring agent for all kinds of foods. The sugar was often pressed into molds and allowed to harden and was then eaten as a candy. Special spring camps in the "sugar bush" were visited annually. Permanent lodges, called "Wig-wa-si-ga-mig" (nicknamed wigwams by the whites) were constructed from poles and recovered each year with hides and bark.

Harvesting techniques were simple but effective. A deep slice was made in the bark of the tree with a knife or tomahawk and a cedar splinter was driven into the wound to serve as a spout. The sap dripped into a birchbark container at the foot of the tree. Before the coming of the trader with his iron kettles, the Indian boiled the sap in clay vessels or by dropping very hot stones into birchbark containers filled with sap. Sugar products were made by slowly stirring the syrup in basswood troughs. Candy was made by pressing the sugar into molds and letting it harden.

In contrast, today's commercial operations are highly sophisticated with miles of plastic tubing carrying the sap from the trees to the processing center. Vacuum systems speed the process and increase the yield.

A family, however, can provide for its own needs by tapping only a few trees and with little investment. Here are some suggestions:

• Select large trees, a least ten inches in diameter. Any of the four varieties of maples which grow in this area will produce sap, but the sugar maple is by far the most productive; it is also sweeter. Do not bother with diseased or rotting trees. If you intend to produce syrup to sell, it will pay to cut out other varieties of trees and any of the smaller maples which may crowd those you tap.* About 80 to 100 trees per acre is considered ideal.

- Sap usually begins to flow in early March when snow is still on the ground but when the temperature rises to about 45°F by day but still falls below freezing at night. The run will usually last from four to six weeks.
- For convenience, tapholes should be about 4½ feet above the ground. Use a 7/16th drill, being careful to make round (not oval) holes so that the sap will not leak around the "spile", as the spigot is called. Tapholes should be about 3" deep for maximum yield. If the drill carries out red sawdust you have gone too deep; you have entered the nonproductive heartwood. The drillings should be white.
- Larger trees may have more than one taphole; here is a rule of thumb:

Maple Syrup Camp, the original "Wigwam".
Courtesy Minnesota Historical Society

* Diseased or rotting trees should also be eliminated.

Indians made syrup by boiling sap for days over an open fire.

Diameter of Tree	Number of Tapholes
10" - 14"	1
15" - 19"	2
20" - 24"	3
25" and larger	4

Avoid drilling into old tapholes.

•Hammer the spiles (they are available commercially) in snugly, but forcing them too hard may cause the bark to split and the tree to leak.

•The life of a taphole may be substantially prolonged by inserting a paraformaldehyde pellet into the hole when it is drilled. This will retard the formation of micro-organisms which multiply rapidly until they reduce the flow of sap or stop it altogether.

•The sap may be collected in pails hung under the spile. Covered containers are available which will help prevent contamination.

•When the sap develops a "buddy" taste, it is time to abandon the tree for that year.

The syrup may be processed out-of-doors as in days gone by over an open wood fire or on a cast-iron stove. Because the evaporation process is a long one, the savings incurred by making your own syrup will be greatly diminished unless the fuel comes from your own woodlot. Commercial processors prefer specially made "sheet pans" to iron kettles because the larger surface permits a more rapid rate of evaporation. The procedure may also be made more efficient by using three containers and ladling the sap from one to the next as it boils, with only the last kettle being used to make the final product.

A cedar spile was traditionally used as the "faucet."
Courtesy Minnesota Historical Society

Make the syrup of a consistence and flavor that best suits your family. The ratio of sap to syrup will usually be somewhere between 28 to 1 and 40 to 1, depending on the sugar content of the sap.

Sugar is made by letting the syrup set and stirring it occasionally after the heat has been removed. The crystals may be pressed into molds and hardened into candy.

Enjoy!

chapter II

WILD RICE

HARVESTING

The Upper Midwest and Ontario have a natural monopoly on wild rice. Small quantities are grown in California and some other parts of Canada, but that amount is relatively insignificant. Wild rice was important to the Indian's diet in this part of the country and was one of the few foods that could be easily and indefinitely stored. Actually, it is not a true rice. In fact, the first French explorers described the grain in their logs as "wild oats". The commercial growers of today use artificial paddies, weed and water control, and have adapted conventional farm machinery to make possible a profitable operation. The University of Minnesota is cooperating with the farmer in developing new strains which are more resistant to wind and hail and which have non-shattering heads which means the grain may be harvested at one time, by machine, in a single operation.

The kernels of rice in the same head of the natural varieties ripen at different times over several days. This is why an area may be harvested several times over a couple of weeks' as new kernels ripen. This is also the reason the law requires the use of canoes or narrow boats so that the rice is not beaten down and wasted, but may be worked several times. There has been no improvement in the harvesting of the non-domestic rice over the method used by the Indians throughout the centuries. The stalks are simply bent over the boat and the ripe kernels are beaten from the head into the boat—usually with stout sticks.

There was also the Indian custom of tying some of the rice into bundles just before it ripened, leaving the plants to continue

The stalks are bent over the boat and the ripe kernels are beaten from the head with a stout stick.

Courtesy Minnesota Historical Society

their growth. These were then harvested as a bundle and this rice had a different flavor and was considered a special delicacy.

PROCESSING

As we have said, for family purposes, the Indian method has not been improved. The harvested rice was parched over or near heat, stirring slowly so that it would not burn. Once the kernels were loosened from the husks, the rice was removed from the

The harvested rice is parched over or near heat, stirring regularly so the kernels will not burn.

Courtesy Minnesota Historical Society

Once the kernels are loosened from the husks, the rice is removed from the heat and pounded.

Courtesy Minnesota Historical Society

heat and pounded. Indians used a large wooden container as a mortar and a pointed post as a pestle. Once the separation was complete, the rice was winnowed by throwing it in the air—over a sheet of birchbark or a blanket—on a windy day. The chaff blew away. As a final step, the last remnants of husks were removed by trampling with clean moccasins. If there were large quantities of rice, the Indians rested their hands or elbows on

Modern day harvesting of wild rice on the Truman Sandland farm near Clearbrook, Minnesota, after the paddies have been drained.

poles secured to either side of a tree. Once again the rice was winnowed; this time the chaff was saved and cooked like rice. The grain could be stored in a cool, dry place—indefinitely.

BASIC RECIPE FOR PREPARING WILD RICE

3 cups of water
1 cup wild rice (washed)—makes 3 cups cooked rice
salt and pepper
1/4 lb. melted butter or margarine

Season water with one tablespoon salt and bring to a boil. Add rice and lower the heat so that the water just simmers. Cook—covered—for about 45 minutes or until the kernels are well opened and the rice is tender. Do not overcook.

Pour off any water that has not been absorbed. Add pepper and a little more salt to taste; pour on the melted butter; and fluff with a fork.

Serve as a side dish or in any of the recipes which follow.

Alternate method:

1 cup wild rice (washed)
4 cups *boiling* water
salt and pepper
1/4 lb. melted butter or margarine

Pour four cups of boiling water over the cup of washed wild rice. Let stand uncovered 20 minutes.

Repeat three times.

Pour off any water that has not been absorbed. Add melted butter; fluff with fork as you salt and pepper to taste.

Another technique is to soak the rice in warm water about four hours.

WILD RICE WITH MUSHROOMS

1 cup wild rice
1/3 cup onions—chopped
1 cup sliced mushrooms (either canned or cooked
    from the wild)
salt and pepper
1/4 lb. butter or margarine

Prepare the wild rice by one of the above methods but do not add butter yet.

Gently fry the chopped onions in the butter (about three minutes or until the onions are "clear").

Add the onions and butter to the rice.

Stir in the mushrooms.

Season lightly as you fluff the rice with a fork.

Serve as a side dish.

Delicious variations of this recipe may be achieved by adding bits of fried bacon and/or chopped celery and/or green pepper. The celery should be fried along with the onions.

WILD RICE AND HAMBURGER HOTDISH[1]

1 cup wild rice (washed)
1 lb. hamburger (beef or
    wild game)
1 large onion, chopped
1 cup celery, chopped

1 small green pepper, chopped
1 small jar pimentos
1 can mushroom soup
1 can water

Prepare the rice by any recipe at the beginning of this section. (1 cup makes three cups cooked rice).

[1]Courtesy Mrs. Donald Hester, Cass Lake, Minnesota.

Fry the hamburger; use a little oil so it will not burn.

When it is about done, add the chopped onion, celery and green pepper. Continue frying for another three or four minutes.

Add pimento, soup and water.

Place in a buttered casserole dish.

Bake 1-1/2 hours in a 300° oven. Add water while baking to prevent dryness.

WILD RICE AND PARTRIDGE [OR PHEASANT] CASSEROLE

    1 cup wild rice (washed)
    flour
    2 partridges or 1 pheasant—deboned and cut up into
        pieces
    1 large onion, chopped
    1 green pepper, chopped
    1 cup celery, chopped
    1 small jar pimentos
    1 can mushroom soup
    1/2 cup sour cream
    1/2 cup water chestnuts
    1/4 cup slivered almonds
    1 can water
    salt and pepper

Cut all of the partridge breast from the bone; cut each half breast into two or three pieces. Pheasant half-breasts may be cut into more pieces because they are larger. Cut the legs and thighs from the carcass. With pheasants, separate the drumstick from the thigh. Season the meat, roll in flour and brown in about 1/3 inch cooking oil.

Prepare the wild rice casserole according to the above recipe for "Wild Rice and Hamburger Hotdish" — leaving out the hamburger.

Add the fried partridge (or pheasant) meat to the casserole; stir in.

Bake in 300° oven for 1-1/2 hours. Add water from time to time to prevent dryness.

If you have leftovers you want to save for another meal, refrigerate. When you are ready to warm it, stir in as much water as necessary to achieve original consistency. Heat for about 1/2 hour in a 300° oven.

Alternate Ingredients

Duck meat goes very well with this recipe. Prebake the ducks until the meat is so well done it is easily picked from the bones.

This may be achieved by roasting the birds in a 300° oven for about three hours in a covered pan with about an inch of water in the bottom or in a "Crockpot" for about 6 hours. An alternate method is to boil the ducks but you will lose some of the flavor (which isn't a bad idea for those who don't care for the "wild taste" of ducks).

LEMON-RUBBED AND WINE-BASTED BAKED FISH WITH WILD RICE DRESSING

Choose a large northern pike, muskie or whitefish. Scale and draw the fish; remove the head, tail, and fins; wash thoroughly inside and out and dry.

Strain the juice of three lemons; salt lightly. Rub the inside and the outside of the fish—thoroughly—with the salted lemon juice. Refrigerate the fish for two or three hours.

Prepare stuffing:
> 1 cup wild rice, washed (will make three cups cooked rice)
> 1/2 cup melted butter or margarine mixed with ½ cup hot water
> 1 large onion, chopped
> 1/3 pound chopped bologna or summer sausage or polish sausage or luncheon meat
> 1 cup celery, chopped
> 1 small green pepper (or ⅓ cup)

Cook the wild rice:
> 3 cups of water
> 1 cup wild rice (washed)
> salt and pepper
> 1/4 lb. melted butter or margarine

Season water with one tablespoon salt and bring to a boil. Add rice and lower the heat so that the water just simmers. Cook—covered—for about 45 minutes or until the kernels are well opened and the rice is tender. Do not overcook.

Pour off any water that has not been absorbed. Add pepper and a little more salt to taste; pour on the melted butter; and fluff with a fork.

Sauté the celery and onions:

Cook slowly in butter or margarine for about three minutes or until the onions are translucent and the celery is light brown.

Combine:

The wild rice, onion, celery, chopped meat and green pepper. Season lightly with salt and pepper. Pour ½ cup melted butter combined with an equal amount of hot water over the mixture and stir the ingredients together—thoroughly.

Stuff and bake:

Pat the chilled fish dry and stuff loosely. Leftover dressing may be baked separately in foil alongside the fish. Place a sheet of foil in the bottom of a roaster, then place the fish in the roaster (back up). Bring the foil up halfway around the fish to hold in the stuffing. Place in a preheated medium oven (350°).

Melt ¼ pound of butter and add an equal amount of white wine. Baste fish from time to time with the wine-butter mixture.

Bake until the meat flakes easily from the large end of the fish (about 15 to 20 minutes per pound).

Transfer baked fish to serving platter; garnish with parsley; and serve with lemon wedges.

WILD RICE—VENISON SAUSAGE CASSEROLE

1½ pounds venison breakfast sausage (Polish or other kinds of link sausage may be substituted, cut into half-inch chunks)
2 large onions
3 envelopes dry onion soup mix
2 cups wild rice (makes 6 cups cooked rice)
3 stalks celery (about 1 cup)
1 cup slivered almonds
1/2 teaspoon garlic powder (optional)
salt and pepper to taste

Prepare the wild rice according to either method described at the beginning of this chapter.

Brown the breakfast sausage. If links are used, cover with water and bring to a boil, then cut into chunks. Chop the onions (coarse) and brown with the sausage or sauté separately if links are used. Meanwhile, prepare the onion soup in seven cups of water, bringing it to a boil.

Using a large, greased casserole dish, add the cooked wild rice and all other ingredients to the soup and stir together. If the mixture seems too dry, add water. Bake, covered, in a 300° oven for one hour. Add water as needed to prevent dryness. Serves eight.

POPPED WILD RICE

Here's a snack that will have your guests guessing!

Wash the wild rice thoroughly, rinsing several times, well in advance of cooking so that it will have time to dry. Preheat cooking oil to 375°. Drop in 2 or 3 tablespoonsful of rice at a time. Remove the popped rice with a large slotted spoon. Salt, add melted butter and serve.

ROAST DUCK WITH WILD RICE STUFFING

See page 55

VENISON AND WILD RICE HASH

1 pound ground venison
1/2 cup wild rice (makes 1½ cups cooked rice)
1 onion, chopped
1 can tomatoes
2 drops Tabasco sauce
salt and pepper to taste

Cook the wild rice by any of the methods described on pages 19 and 20.

Brown the hamburger and onions together in a skillet (use a little cooking oil). Add the cooked wild rice to the hamburger and onions; also add the tomatoes and 2 drops of Tabasco sauce. If it appears too dry, add a little water. Stir all ingredients together as you continue to fry over low heat for about ten minutes. Season with salt and pepper to taste.

Serve with eggs.

WILD RICE PANCAKES

Cook 1/3 cup wild rice; this should make about 1 full cup cooked rice.

Prepare enough batter according to your favorite recipe for about 50 medium size (4") pancakes.

Stir in the cooked wild rice and fry on a hot griddle.

chapter III

MORE FROM YOUR GAME ANIMALS

Assuming you are a hunter, this chapter is written to help you more fully enjoy your trophies and to call to your attention certain animals and cuts often overlooked. Wild game in its prime—well cared for and properly prepared—should be more palatable than the most expensive cuts found in the supermarket meat counter. Expect, and enjoy, a different flavor. With wild game, much good meat is often wasted and the tougher cuts, especially those from older animals, are endured rather than enjoyed. Small game is often ignored, both as a source of hunting pleasure and good eating.

Special recipes and special treatments will help turn even the less enthusiastic members of your family into wild game connoisseurs.

CARE AND PRESERVATION OF GAME

The best gourmet recipes cannot compensate for improper care and preservation of game animals. A few basic rules apply regardless of size, whether your trophy is a squirrel or a moose.

- Contrary to popular belief, large game animals need not always be bled. If the shot has entered the chest cavity, chances are there will be adequate internal bleeding which will drain as you clean out the abdominal and chest areas. However, with a spine, gut or neck shot, it is a good idea to cut a neck artery before proceeding to dress out the animal.
- Clean out the entrails just as soon as possible after the kill. It is important that body heat be reduced quickly. If water is available, use it. If the animal was "gut shot" or if body

fluids stained the meat and if the water does not do the job, cut away the affected areas.

- As you make the incision, take your time and be careful not to cut into the intestines. As you remove the entrails, be especially careful that you do not rupture the bladder or lower bowel track. Extend the incision well up the neck so that all of the lungs, windpipe and esophagus can be easily removed.
- Cut the "aitch" bone between the legs with a stout knife, saw or axe.
- Save the heart and liver. You may also want to try other seldom used parts such as the tongue, kidneys, meat from the nose of the moose, etc. Early Indians and some Eskimos and northern Indians of today relish other parts. For example, fresh tripe is eaten raw immediately after slaughter, preferably with a little salt and pepper.
- When you have finished cleaning out the animal, prop the body cavity open with a stick so as to further facilitate heat escapement.
- Hang the animal head up. The flavor of the meat will be enhanced and the cuts will be considerably more tender if allowed to hang several days: 2 days for a small deer, 4 days for a big buck and 5 days or more for a caribou, elk or moose. If the animal has been quartered in order to haul it out of the woods, no problem—hang the quarters. Choose a cool, dry place free from flies. Just above freezing to 50° F. is ideal.

BUTCHERING

When cutting up your animal, take the time to do a good job. If it is your first experience, seek out a friend who is skilled in meat cutting to teach you. This will mean not only better quality but much less waste. If you would like to try it on your own, here are some helpful hints:

- Hang the deer, head down.
- Skin the animal, starting with the hindquarters. Although a knife is a necessary tool in the skinning process, time can be saved by grasping the hide firmly with both hands and pulling down with a sharp, quick motion.
- Using a meat saw, split the carcass into two halves by cutting through the length of the backbone.
- Remove the pot roasts on either side of the neck.
- Lay half the carcass on a work table, inside down.

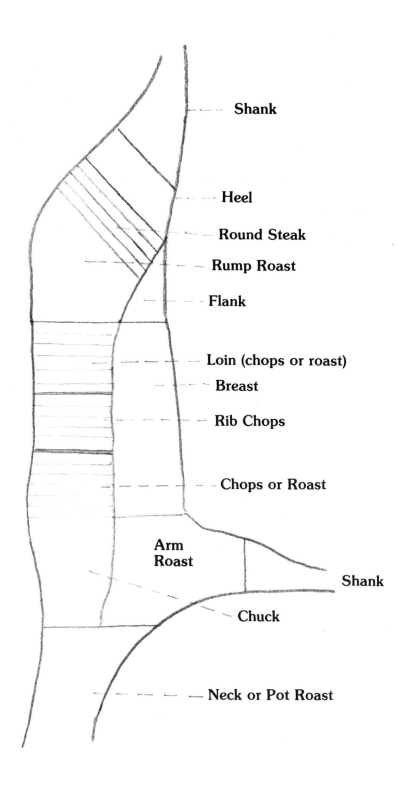

Shank

Heel

Round Steak

Rump Roast

Flank

Loin (chops or roast)

Breast

Rib Chops

Chops or Roast

Arm
Roast

Shank

Chuck

Neck or Pot Roast

- Remove the hindquarter by cutting along the backbone and then down into the socket, completely separating the quarter from the carcass. The rump roast at the top of the quarter may be removed by a cut parallel to the "aitch bone".
- Remove the shank at the narrow end of the quarter. This is best used for hamburger.
- Cut the balance of the round into steaks, about 1 inch thick, being careful to make clean, parallel cuts, then sawing through the bone.
- Remove the front quarter by pulling the leg away from the body and cutting the tissue as you pull, working toward the backbone.
- Cut away the front shank and save for hamburger.
- The remainder of the front quarter may be cut into arm roasts.
- The top of the shoulder is used as a chuck roast.
- Remove the flank.
- Remove the "breast meat" and save for hamburger.
- Cut across (saw) the ribs, about two inches from the backbone, starting at the front (head) end of the loin. Rib chops may then be cut from the front end of the loin and loin chops from the rear end; they may also be cut as roasts.
- Ribs may be baked or barbecued or the meat may be saved for hamburger.

Carefully remove all hairs from the meat. Cut away all damaged parts. Bloody areas can often be salvaged by soaking the meat overnight in a salt solution; 1/2 pound salt to 1 gallon water. Save all cuttings and trimmings for hamburger and sausage. However, in most cases, far too much prime meat ends up in the grinder. For example, tough roasts can be slow-baked and, if they are still not tender, used in combination with vegetables as an excellent stew. Rib meat is especially flavorful, yet most butchers just trim it off the bone for hamburger. Your family will receive much greater pleasure if you bake them with barbecue sauce. Do not cut your steaks too thin; they will tend to dry out when you prepare them. You may have your own preference, but if in doubt, try between 3/4 inch and 1 inch thick for a starter.

Package the cuts the right size for your family. Double wrap all meat in quality freezer paper, tightly, so as to squeeze out all air and prevent freezer burn. Sharp freeze the meat in the coldest spot in your freezer. Maintaining constant temperature in your freezer is important in keeping food for long periods of time.

Even with the kind of care described in this chapter, quality will diminish after a few months. For best eating, make a habit of consuming all game within one year from the time it is shot.

Smaller animals, such as rabbits and squirrels, may be kept fresher longer by freezing the cuts in water to seal out the air.

TENDERIZING AND MARINADES

Commercial tenderizers are a familiar market item. They work quite well but may alter the flavor. Marinades also change the flavor and may or may not be to your taste, so experiment until you find the treatment that pleases you and your family.

WINE VINEGAR-WORCESTERSHIRE-SOY SAUCE MARINADE
The following ingredients will treat enough steak for a family of four:

2 tablespoons cooking oil
1 tablespoon Worcestershire sauce
1 tablespoon soy sauce
1/2 cup red wine vinegar
1/2 teaspoon salt

Combine all ingredients, pour over steaks or chops. Let stand overnight, under refrigeration, turning as you have the opportunity. Piercing the meat will speed the tenderizing process.

CITRUS-CIDER MARINADE
The following ingredients are sufficient to treat a 6 to 8 pound roast;

3 lemons, juice
1 large orange, juice
2 cups cider
1/2 cup vinegar
1 medium onion—chopped
3 stalks celery, chopped
1/2 teaspoon nutmeg

Combine all ingredients. Place roast in pan and pour marinade over the meat. Turn several times during treatment. If you suspect the roast is really tough, let stand up to 3 days under refrigeration or in a cool place. Marinade may be used to baste roast while it is being cooked.

CLOVE MARINADE

15 whole cloves
8 bay leaves
8 peppercorns
1 large onion, chopped
1 cup white vinegar or cooking wine
1 cup water

Marinate steaks and chops by turning at least twice during a 24 hour period. Keep under refrigeration. Roasts should be turned or basted as convenient. Marinate up to three days for tough roasts.

South Seas Marinated Steak[1]

Two pounds of steaks—¾ to 1 inch thick. If wild game is used, trim off fat.

Marinating Sauce
1/2 cup salad oil
2 tablespoons soy sauce
1/4 cup sugar
1/4 cup finely chopped onion
1/2 tablespoon salt, 1/2 tablespoon pepper
4 tablespoons sesame seed

Place steaks in a shallow dish or pan. Cover with marinade. Let stand overnight[2] in refrigerator.

If the sauce does not cover the steaks, brush surface generously and then turn steaks over in the morning.

Broil steaks over charcoal or under broiler. Baste with sauce.

TOUGH MEAT RECIPES

Don't despair if that trophy buck of a lifetime chews like "old ironsides". The flavor is still there; all you need is a little different treatment to make it enjoyable. First, you may want to try the tenderizing techniques just discussed; those failing, try some of the following recipes. If they don't work, give up and make hamburger or sausage of the rest of your animal!

Tenderized Steak (Cube Steak)

Round steak is often tougher than other cuts and is a good candidate for this treatment.

---

[1]Courtesy Mrs. Ralph Dokken, Evergreen, Colorado.

[2]If you suspect the steaks may be tough, let stand 24 hours.

Sprinkle a liberal portion of flour over each steak and vigorously pound it into the meat. Ideally, you should use a mallet designed for the job, however, the butt end of a knife will do the trick. Turn the steaks over and repeat.

Now fry the steaks on a hot griddle or in a hot pan lightly coated with oil. They will get done quickly—about four or five minutes to the side if they are about a half inch thick.

Baked Steak

Bake only the tougher cuts of wild game. Save your choice, tender cuts for broiling or frying. Use 3/4 to 1 inch steaks (trim off fat).

MUSHROOM STYLE

Arrange the steaks in a single layer in a baking dish or oven pan. A skillet will do, providing it does not have a wood or plastic handle. Season lightly with salt and pepper.

Cover the steaks with mushroom soup. One 26 oz. can of soup plus one can of water will cover two pounds of steaks. Be sure the liquid covers the meat.

Cover the pan or dish. If you do not have a cover that fits, use foil. Place in preheated, 300° oven. Bake for two hours.

SWISS STEAK (Tomato style)

 2 pounds round steak (if wild game, trim away fat)
 1 26 oz. can (large) tomato soup
 1 can water
 1 cup chopped celery
 1 large sliced onion
 1 small, sliced green pepper
 salt and pepper

Season steaks and arrange in single layer in baking dish or pan.

Add chopped celery, sliced onion and sliced green pepper.

Cover with soup mixture (tomato soup and equal amount of water). Be sure meat is covered by liquid. If you prefer a spicier sauce, add catsup or a couple of drops of Tabasco sauce. Place in preheated, 300° oven for two hours.

BAKED STEAK WITH ONION SOUP MIX

Ideal for tougher cuts of wild game. Trim away fat.
Use 3/4 to 1 inch cuts.
Lay steaks on foil. Place generous pats of margarine or butter

here and there on steaks; about one quarter pound in all for 2 pounds of steak—evenly.

Bring the foil over the steaks and seal on top.

Place in preheated 250° oven for two hours.

The onion soup mix may be saved and poured into a bowl and mixed with an equal amount of hot water—then used as a gravy or poured over the steaks.

This is also an excellent way to prepare steaks that have been in your freezer several months (even a year). But first trim away any freezer burn.

Pot Roast

Trim fat from the roast.

Rub in salt and pepper—you may also want to try garlic salt.

Roll the roast in flour and brown all sides in cooking oil.

Add about one-half cup of water, cover tightly and cook slowly for two and one-half to three hours (275° to 300° oven). A "Dutch Oven" on top of the stove also works well.

For a true pot roast dinner, add whole small onions, carrots and whole, peeled small potatoes the last hour.

TO KEEP ROASTS TENDER AND JUICY

Never let the interior meat temperature exceed 170° F.

STEW
(Beef, Venison, Elk, Caribou, Moose, Etc.)

Since it takes so long to prepare a stew "from scratch", we are going to cheat a little! We will use canned beef stew as a base and a roast instead of regular stew meat. There just isn't enough meat in most canned stews to satisfy a hungry man.

Four servings: 2 cans of beef stew (24 oz. cans)
1 can mixed vegetables (#2 can)
1 large can tomato soup (26 oz. can)
1-1/2 to 2 pounds of wild game roast, cut into bite-size portions. (Leftover roast makes great stew meat)

Prepare roast according to instructions for pot roast above. Medium doneness is best for stew meat, but be sure it is tender. The crockpot is a good tenderizer.

Empty the contents of the cans of beef stew, mixed vegetables and tomato soup into an iron kettle or deep iron skillet. Stir in pre-cooked meat chunks.

Simmer over open flame, on top of stove or in a low oven

(250°) for 40 minutes; stir occasionally.

For a spicier stew, add 1/2 cup catsup and/or a few drops of Tabasco sauce.

Stew From Scratch

2 pounds chuck or pot roast (any big game) cut into 1 inch cubes
1 large onion, chopped (coarse)
1 pound small, whole sweet onions
1 large can tomato soup (24 oz.)
1 can V-8 juice (12 oz.)
1 tablespoon salt
6 whole black peppers
8 medium carrots (sliced)
1 package frozen peas
2 pounds small or cut potatoes
2 cups water

Brown the cubed meat in cooking oil over low heat. Add water and bring to a boil. Add tomato soup, V-8 juice, meat chunks, sliced onion, salt and peppers; let simmer for two hours. Add small onions, carrots, potatoes and peas and cook covered for about 30 minutes or until the vegetables are done. For spicier stew, add 1/2 cup catsup.

Depression Stew[1]

During the Great Depression of the 1930's this recipe was developed on the Iron Range of Minnesota. Wieners were very cheap in those days and were used as a "steak extender". Nowadays, the steak "extends the wieners"!

Four servings:

1 lb. round steak (beef, venison or other wild game) —cut lean meat into one inch squares.
1 lb. wieners—cut into 1/2 inch slices.
1 cup catsup
1 cup water
1 large sliced onion
salt and pepper
1/2 cup celery, chopped
1/4 cup green pepper, chopped
1/2 cup brown sugar

[1]Courtesy Mike Matanich, Staples, Minnesota.

1 T oregano
1 t garlic salt

Season the beef or venison squares with salt and pepper. Cover meat chunks with water and let simmer 30 minutes. Add onions, celery and green pepper and continue cooking another 30 minutes or until meat is tender.

Add catsup, brown sugar, spices and water (blend).

You may need to add water to keep meat covered.

Once steak is tender, add wiener chunks and continue simmering another 10 minutes.

Serve over boiled or mashed potatoes, rice or noodles.

Once you've tried this hearty dish you may feel the depression wasn't so tough after all!

(For a spicier meal, add 1 T. Worchestershire sauce or a drop or two of Tabasco.)

RABBITS AND SQUIRRELS

With all of the game available in the Upper Midwest and Ontario, many hunters overlook the sport and good eating these small game animals have to offer. In fact, in many parts of the United States, these are about the only animals available to hunt and it is for this reason that rabbits and squirrels head the list of game taken in the United States each year.

Baked Squirrel

4 squirrels, dressed but left whole
2 large onions, quartered
1 large onion, sliced
4 slices bacon—the fatter the better
salt and pepper inside and out.

Place in baking dish, side by side, back sides up on top of the quartered onions. In other words, stuff the body cavities with onion as best you can. Cut bacon slices in two and place on backs of squirrels alternately with onion slices. Cover and bake in 350° oven between 1½ and 2 hours or until tender.

Fried Cottontail Rabbit

Cottontails are the most tender of rabbits and can be successfully prepared by most any of the following recipes.

Dissect the rabbit as you would a chicken. Roll in seasoned flour and fry slowly in butter until well browned on all sides. If you feel the meat is not going to be sufficiently tender, cover with water and bring to a boil, then lower heat and let simmer for 1 hour or until tender.

Snowshoe Pie

1 rabbit, dressed and cut into bite-size chunks
2 cans mixed vegetables, drained
1 can small, whole potatoes, drained
baking powdered biscuits (from scratch or your grocer's dairy case)

Marinate rabbit overnight in salt water. If there is no time for this, rub all parts with a solution of vinegar and water.

Debone and cut into bite-size chunks. Dredge in seasoned flour and brown slowly in butter. Place in greased baking dish with mixed vegetables and small potatoes. Lightly salt and pepper and stir mixture together. Place baking powder biscuits on top of stew mixture, sides touching. Bake in a 300° oven until biscuits are done.

Jack Rabbit Mushroom Casserole

1 large Jack rabbit
2 cans mushroom soup
1 oz. can mushroom stems and pieces

Marinate the rabbit in salt water overnight. Dissect into pieces. Dredge in seasoned flour and brown over low heat. Place pieces in a greased casserole. Cover with mushroom soup, adding enough water to completely cover all pieces of meat. Add the mushroom stems and pieces. Bake in a 325° oven (covered) for 1½ hours or until tender.

German Hasenpfeffer

2 snowshoe or cottontail rabbits
1/2 cup cooking oil
1 cup cooking wine
2 onions, sliced
1 tablespoon allspice
1 teaspoon salt, a couple of dashes of pepper
1/4 cup flour
2 tablespoons sugar

Cut the rabbits into pieces as you would a chicken. Make a marinade of the oil, wine, onions, allspice, salt, and pepper. Cover meat; cover dish; refrigerate and marinate for two days. Drain on paper towel, but save marinade. Dredge meat in seasoned flour and brown in cooking oil. Remove rabbit and pour off all oil and fats. Return meat to pan and cover with marinade, adding sugar. Bring to a boil, then reduce heat and simmer until tender (about 45 min. to 1 hour).

Rabbit and Dumplings

2 rabbits, dissected

Dredge the rabbit pieces in seasoned flour and sear in cooking oil in a hot skillet. Cover with hot water and add the following seasonings:

2 bay leaves
1 pinch thyme
1 teaspoon celery salt
8 peppercorns

While the stew is simmering, make dumplings from bisquick mix according to the recipe on the box. Add the dumplings to the stew and let simmer until both the rabbit and the dumplings are done.

Spicy Rabbit

Guaranteed to be tender and tasty:

1 chicken bouillon cube dissolved in 1 cup boiling water
1/4 cup lemon juice
1 cup orange juice
1 small can mushrooms
1 green pepper, sliced
1 tbsp. parsley flakes
1 pinch ginger

Disjoint the rabbit as you would a chicken. Season lightly with salt and pepper and dredge in flour. Brown in oil, preferably bacon grease. Add bouillon, juices, green pepper, parsley, mushrooms and ginger. If this does not cover rabbit pieces, add enough water to do so. Cover and simmer until meat is tender (about 1½ hours).

Other Ways to Fix Squirrel and Rabbit

Bake the animals in a slow oven until they are so well done the meat may be easily separated from the bone. (You may use a Crock-pot.) Cut the meat into small pieces and then use with your favorite stew or casserole recipe.[4]

ENJOYING LESS POPULAR GAME ANIMALS AND MEAT CUTS

Some animals cherished by the Indian for their flavor are no longer thought of as a source of good eating, either because

[4] See Wild Rice recipes.

they may no longer be hunted legally or because they have gone out of style. Beaver and muskrat are in that first category and although they may not be hunted, they may be trapped in season. If you are not a trapper yourself, get next to someone who is and give roast beaver or fried muskrat a try.

Here are a couple of recipes:

Roast Beaver

    1 young beaver (10# or under)
    4 onions, 2 whole and 2 sliced
    1 cup red cooking wine
    1/2 cup vinegar
    6 strips bacon or sidepork

Dress animal; remove all fat. Add vinegar to 2 cups water and wash beaver thoroughly. Marinate 2 days in salt water solution. Pat dry. Place in roaster. Cut two whole onions in half and place in body cavity. Slice other 2 onions and lay on beaver—alternating with strips of bacon or sidepork. Place cooking wine plus 1/2 cup water in bottom of roaster. Cover and bake for about 20 minutes for each pound of animal or until very tender so that the meat can be easily removed from the bone. Strip all meat from the carcass and serve on a warm platter.

Beaver Tail

The tail contains a surprising amount of meat. It may be roasted with the rest of the animal or prepared separately, but first, it must be skinned!

This meat is normally not very tender. You may parboil it in seasoned water for 30 minutes or marinate it overnight in a solution of 1/2 cup of vinegar, 1 tablespoon salt and enough water to cover the tail.

If you prefer to fry the tail, cut it into serving size pieces, season with salt and pepper, dredge in flour and fry slowly in a combination of cooking oil and butter or margarine.

For gourmet treatment, once the meat has been browned, add the following to the skillet:

    1/2 cup red cooking wine
    1 can of mushroom pieces (4 oz.)
    1 medium onion, choped
    enough water to cover the meat

Let simmer 20 minutes or until tender. Serve garnished with mushrooms.

By cutting the tail into smaller pieces, this makes a delightful hors d'oeuvres recipe. (Serve hot)

Breakfast Beaver[5]

Debone the beaver quarters.
Slice steaks thin, cross grain, about 1/4 inch thick.
Roll steaks in bisquick flour, seasoned with salt and pepper.
Fry in Crisco. Use low heat until almost done, then turn up to high for the final minute.
Serve with pancakes or French toast.

Muskrat

Muskrat may be prepared according to any of the squirrel or rabbit recipes in this section. When the animal has been skinned, remove all fat and wipe with a solution of vinegar and water (1 to 3). Let soak 24 hours under refrigeration in a salt and water solution. If you fry it, use plenty of chopped onion in the pan and if you happen to have an older animal which seems tough even after frying, cover the meat with water, bring to a boil and then simmer until the meat can be easily removed from the bone.

Roast Raccoon—3 Ways

You have probably heard some swear that raccoon is the finest game animal to be found on this continent, while others insist their experience with the animal was "just awful". The difference in their evaluation probably lies with one or more of the following causes:
- Older and larger animals tend to be strong.
- All of the fat may not have been removed.
- The bean-shaped glands under each leg may not have been removed.

The moral of the story is to choose young animals (4-6 pounds), cut away all visible fat and remove the glands from under the legs before preparing. It will also help to give the dressed carcass a vinegar and water bath and let soak in salt water under refrigeration overnight.

One traditional way to prepare raccoon is to barbecue the animal whole over an open fire or charcoal, on a spit. Allow plenty of time (three to four hours depending on the size of the animal) and baste occasionally (every half hour) with your favorite barbecue sauce.

If you prefer to roast the animal, cut into serving size pieces, season with salt and pepper, dredge in flour and brown over low

[5]Courtesy Mrs. Trixie Wyant, Aitkin, Minnesota.

heat in cooking oil. Add a chopped onion to the pan during the frying process. Transfer the browned pieces to a roaster. Lay onion slices and pieces of bacon over the meat. Bake in a 325° oven for 2 to 3 hours or until tender.

A third alternative is to season the whole carcass of a small raccoon inside and out, stuff with your favorite dressing and bake in a covered roaster with pieces of bacon or salt pork draped over the "breast". Again, use medium heat and roast until the meat can easily be removed from the bone.

LEG OF PORCUPINE

For many years porcupine were protected on the theory that a lost hunter could catch and kill the slow moving creatures easily and thus escape starvation. Because of the damage these animals do to trees, they have been taken off the protective list in many areas. Check local game laws, however, before killing one.

Use the legs only. Skin and trim away all fat.

Soak in cold, salted water overnight, to which 2 tablespoons of vinegar have been added.

Drain and pat dry.

Season lightly with salt and pepper, dredge in flour, and brown in oil (preferably part or all bacon grease).

Place in an iron kettle; cover with onion slices. Using some of the drippings from the frying process, add flour and water to make a gravy. Pour this over the porcupine, cover, and let simmer until tender (2 to 3 hours). Baste occasionally with the gravy.

Save Those Big Game Ribs - They're Too Good For Hamburger!

Cut the ribs into 3 inch lengths, leaving them joined together by the meat in between. Cover them with water seasoned with salt. Bring to a boil, then lower heat and let simmer for one hour.

Meanwhile, prepare the following sweet and sour sauce:

3/4 cup sugar	juice of one lemon
1/2 cup cider vinegar	1 teaspoon soy sauce
1/4 cup catsup	1/4 cup cornstarch dissolved
1/2 cup water	in 1/4 cup water

Combine sugar, vinegar, catsup, water and lemon juice in sauce pan. Cook over medium heat 3 to 4 minutes. Stir in soy sauce and dissolve cornstarch. Bring to a boil, stirring constantly. Cook until thick and clear.

Drain the water from the ribs. Pour the sweet and sour sauce over the ribs and cook over low heat for another 15 minutes—turning the ribs so that all meat is well covered with the sauce.

Ribs may also be baked. Prepare them in a roaster in a 300° oven for 2 to 3 hours or until tender. They are especially delicious basted with your favorite barbecue sauce. If you do not use sauce, season the ribs before baking with salt and pepper.

BEAR RECIPES

Black Bear can be very good eating—but it can also be tough. It is important that bear meat always be *well done*. The same disease that sometimes effects pork, Trichinosis, has been known to be found in bear as well. Take no chances.

Always remove as much fat as possible when preparing any cut of bear meat. It tends to be fat anyway. Actually, bear fat is very white and may be rendered into excellent lard. It is especially good for frying donuts.

Bear Chops and Steaks—

Prepare them the same as you would pork chops or pork steaks. If the bear is relatively young, the chops and steaks are excellent fried. If the animal is on the tough side, try baking according to this recipe:

Use thick or "double chops". Trim away all the fat. Season the chops, then brown both sides. Prepare wild rice stuffing according to the recipe on page 22. Place the stuffing in a baking dish or roaster. "Submerge" the chops in the dressing. Cover and place in a preheated 300° oven for 1½ hrs. Be sure the chops are tender and well done, all the way through.

Tough Steak—

Try any of the three recipes for baked steak on page 31.

Bear Roast—

Trim away all the fat. Rub with a vinegar-water solution (1 to 3). Pat dry. Season with pepper and garlic salt (or regular salt if you prefer). Roll the roast in flour and brown on all sides in cooking oil.

Add about 1/2 cup water and 1/2 cup red cooking wine (optional). Cover tightly and cook slowly until well done—about 3 hours at 300°. A few onion slices baked on top of the roast will also add to the flavor.

VENISON MINCE MEAT (FOR PIES)

For six pies:

1 pound venison (any roast cut)
1/2 pound beef suet, chopped fine
4 cups apple cider
1 orange, use both the juice and the grated rind
1 lemon, juice of
6 medium apples, hard variety
1 pound dried currants
1 pound raisins
1/4 pound candied fruit cake mix
3 cups brown sugar
1 tablespoons nutmeg
1 teaspoon allspice
1 dash ginger
1 teaspoon cinnamon
1/2 tablespoon cloves
1 teaspoon salt

Roast the venison until tender (or use left over meat from a roast). Chop fine. Add all other ingredients and mix thoroughly, being especially careful to mix as the spices are being added to insure uniform taste. Use your favorite pie crust recipe.

LIVER WITH ONIONS AND BACON

In many deer camps, fresh, fried liver with onions and bacon is tradition at the end of the first day of hunting. Liver is never better than when fresh, but it may be frozen for up to a month or two without losing too much in quality.

Four servings:

2 lb. liver, sliced thin (1/2 inch)(of any big game animal)
2 large onions, sliced
8 thick slices bacon
1 small can (2 oz.) sliced mushrooms
or 1/2 cup chopped fresh mushrooms
1 cup flour
salt and pepper

Wash the liver and trim away any tissue that may still be attached. Large livers from older animals may have a tough, outside "skin" which should be removed. Small livers from young animals are best.

Cut liver into fairly thin slices—about 1/3 to 1/2 inch thick.

Season the sliced liver and roll in flour, covering both sides.

Start the bacon while you are preparing the liver. After there is enough melted fat in the pan, add the onion slices and mushrooms. When the bacon is done, remove from pan.

Add the liver and fry with the onions. If onions start to burn, remove. Liver fries quickly—use medium heat. Overcooking may make it tough, so test with knife as it is frying on the second side (about 5 minutes a side).

Return bacon to pan (also onions if they have been removed) the last couple of minutes to reheat. Drain bacon on paper towel before serving.

LIVERWURST (mock smoked liver sausage)

1# sliced liver
1 onion—sliced
1 carrot—sliced
1/4 teaspoon fresh ground black peppercorns
1/2 tablespoon garlic salt
2 tablespoons salt (level)
2 tablespoons wheat germ
powdered milk
1 tablespoon smoke flavoring or hickory sauce

Sauté the onion slices until transparent (preferably in bacon grease). Add liver, carrots, pepper and garlic (and more oil if necessary) and cook until liver is cooked and carrots are soft (about 10 or 12 minutes). Run the mixture through a meat grinder two or three times until smooth and well blended. Add the remaining ingredients, using enough powdered milk to make a firm mixture. Wrap in plastic or sausage casings and refrigerate. Use as a paste on crackers or slice as a sandwich meat.

HEART AND WILD RICE

1 cup wild rice (makes 3 cups cooked rice)
1/3 cup chopped onion
1 cup sliced mushrooms or stems and pieces
1/4 pound butter
1 small, big game heart

Cut the heart in half. Remove all fat, tubes, etc. Cut into small pieces. Meanwhile, prepare the wild rice according to any of the recipes on pages 19-20.

Sauté the heart pieces and onion in butter over low heat for about 4 minutes. Add the rice and mushrooms and season with salt and pepper as you stir the ingredients together. Cook over low heat until the heart pieces are well done.

Big game heart may also be baked. Use pepper, salt, garlic and bay leaves for seasoning.

STUFFED HEART

For two small or 1 large big game heart: clean hearts, slice open and remove arteries, veins, and fat. Prepare stuffing from any recipe in this book such as found on page 22. Stuff heart and close opening with skewers. Roll in seasoned flour and brown in cooking oil (slowly). Bake in medium oven (330°) for 1½ hours. Slice and serve.

HEART LUNCHEON MEAT

Open heart; remove fats and tissues. Wash clean.
Place the heart in a kettle and cover with water.
Add:
    1 bay leaf
    1/2 cup chopped celery
    1 onion, sliced
Let the heart simmer until it is tender throughout (about 2 hours).
Let cool and slice for sandwiches or as cold cuts.

FRIED HEART

Fresh heart may be sliced and fried the same as liver. It is especially good with onions and bacon.

PICKLED TONGUE (OR HEART)

For 4 to 6 deer tongues:
    1 pt. vinegar
    1 pt. water
    2 tablespoons sugar
    1 teaspoon whole cloves
    1 teaspoon whole allspice
    1 teaspoon whole black peppers
    1/2 teaspoon mustard seed
    1/2 teaspoon salt

Wash tongues in salted water. Place in fresh water. Add 1 tablespoon allspice, and let simmer one to two hours or until tender. (It will never get real tender.) Let cool and peel off skin and cut off root ends. Place in jars and submerge in a pickling solution prepared from the above ingredients which has been boiled for about 10 minutes.
Refrigerate and let stand one week before eating.

MOOSE HEART STEW

You may use any big game heart, but will have to vary the amounts of ingredients added to achieve the stew consistency you prefer.

Clean the heart, removing all fat and the inside tissues and large vessels. Cut into bite-sized pieces.

Coat the pieces with seasoned flour and brown over medium heat—do not let the pieces get crusty.

Add the meat to your favorite stew ingredients or try the following for a starter:

> 1 large onion, sliced and sautéed with the heart meat 3 or 4 minutes before adding it to the stew
> 1 cup celery, diced and sautéed along with the onion; do not burn
> 1 can mushrooms or 1 cup uncooked mushrooms
> 2 cans mixed vegetables or cook your choices of raw vegetables
> 1 large can tomato soup
> 1 large can tomatoes (if the tomatoes are whole, cut into bite-sized pieces)
> 2 bay leaves

Season to taste with salt and pepper or soup seasonings.

For a zestier stew, add catsup or 2 drops Tabasco sauce.

If the stew is too thick, add a little water or a small can of tomato soup.

Let simmer for about 30 minutes. If you used raw vegetables or mushrooms, let simmer until all vegetables are done.

SPICED TONGUE

For two small or one large tongue taken from big game.

> 1 tablespoon salt
> 4 whole black peppers
> 6 whole cloves
> 4 whole allspice
> 1 bay leaf (large)
> 1 tablespoon vinegar
> 1 small onion, sliced

Cover tongues with water. Simmer for one hour. Add all other ingredients and simmer for another hour or two until tender. Cool. Slit skin on underside of tongues and peel off. Slice on a slant. Excellent as sandwich meat or cold cut.

HEAD CHEESE

This tasty delicacy receives its name from the fact the pork used traditionally came from a hog's head. You may still use that source for this recipe, but hogs' heads may be a little hard to come by in your local market!

But here is an old favorite Scandinavian recipe and a good way to use your venison:

  2 lbs. venison shank or roast meat
  2 lbs. pork shoulder roast or lean meat from a hog's head
  10 allspice
  5 bay leaves
  1 teaspoon garlic salt
  1 teaspoon white pepper
  3 tablespoons brown sugar
  2 onions, sliced (medium)
  2 tablespoons salt

Chop both the venison and the pork into small pieces (about ½ bite-size).

Place in a crockpot and cover with water. Let simmer on low until very tender (about 4-5 hours).

Place the meat in a dishtowel; tie with a string; and place in a stone crock or other non-metallic container.

Make a spice-brine by adding the spices and brown sugar as listed above to enough water to cover the meat. Boil briefly, stirring continuously. Pour the solution over the meat.

Place a board on top of the meat and press down firmly. Place a clean rock on top of the board to maintain pressure.

Store in a cool place or under refrigeration. Wait a couple of days and then slice cold to serve—with vinegar on the side.

RULLEPOLSE (Scandinavian meat roll)

Flank meat or other relatively thin "sheets" of meat that can be rolled are usually used. Meat scraps that would normally be used for stew meat (or hamburger) are also used (not tough pieces however). All meat should be boneless.

Lay the flank meat flat. Spread the scraps (bite-sized) evenly over the flank meat. Season lightly with salt and pepper. Sprinkle 1/3 teaspoon ginger to each pound of meat. Chop a large onion and sprinkle over meat. Roll and wrap tightly with string.

Prepare a brine solution with enough water to cover the meat. Use enough salt to float an egg or a potato. Add 1/2 teaspoon saltpeter per gallon of water. Boil until the salt dissolves.

When the brine has cooled, place the meat roll in a non-metallic container and cover with the solution. Place a weight on top to keep the meat totally submerged. Let soak in cool place 48 hours. Remove and soak overnight in fresh water in a cool place.

Remove and place in fresh water again and boil slowly for two hours.

Place meat in loaf pan; force to fit. Use more than one pan and cut meat to fit if necessary. Store in cool place with weight on top to hold shape.

Slice thin and serve cold.

JELLIED MOOSE NOSE

The nose of the moose has long been considered a delicacy by Native Americans. Early white settlers also enjoyed it—usually roasted.

Use the nose, cutting off the upper jaw bone just under the eyes. Boil in a large kettle for 45 minutes. Cool. Now the hair may be easily removed.

Submerge the nose in fresh water. Add a chopped onion and two tablespoons pickling spices and 1 bay leaf. Let simmer until tender.

Cool overnight in the same liquid.

Remove the bone and cartilage. You will find the bulb of the nose contains white meat. The thin strips along the bones and jowls will be dark. Slice both the light and dark meat, thin. Pack in jars and cover with the liquid in which the nose was boiled. The liquid will jell when kept in a cool place.

Slice the meat and serve cold.

BIG GAME SALAMI

Scrap cuts of big game meat make excellent salami (summer sausage). Vary the seasonings called for until they suit your own taste. You can make it stronger or milder by controlling the use of garlic salt, smoked salt, pepper or liquid smoke. Try these proportions for a starter:

     5 pounds ground venison or other big game
     1 pound ground pork (quite fat)
     3 tablespoons mustard seed
     2 tablespoons ground peppercorns
       (measured after grinding)
     3 teaspoons garlic salt
     4 tablespoons curing salt
     2 tablespoons liquid smoke

Mix all ingredients *thoroughly.*

Work into rolls the size you prefer. Bake in low oven (170-180°). The length of time will depend on the diameter of the meat roll, varying from 8 hours for 2 inches to 12 hours for 4 inches. Lay meat on a rack over a drip pan or aluminum foil to catch drippings. Sample occasionally to see if it is done to your liking. Wrap in plastic or stuff into sausage casing and store under refrigeration or freeze for future enjoyment.

Instead of using smoke flavoring (such as smoke salt or liquid smoke), you may choose to smoke the meat instead of baking it.

SAUSAGE

> 20 pounds dressed wild game
> 10 pounds fat pork (this amount will vary with taste, but unless you use at least this weight of fat pork the sausage will be dry)
> 2 teaspoons sugar
> 1 teaspoon ginger
> 1/2 pound fine salt
> 2 tablespoons pepper
> 1 tablespoon sage

Cut the meat up into small pieces which can be easily fed into a grinder. Run the meat through the grinder twice. To assure uniform seasoning, place the ground meat into five or more piles and work the proportionate amount of seasoning in with your hands. Form into patties and refrigerate or divide into approximately 1 pound quantities, wrap in freezer paper and freeze.

SMOKED SAUSAGE (Links)

Use the same recipe as for sausage, but omit the sugar and ginger. Instead, add 1½ ounces saltpeter and increase the sage to 1 cup. If you like "hot" sausage, chop *fine* 1/2 ounce red pepper pods.

Place the ground meat in five or more piles and work in the proportionate amount of seasoning with your hands to insure uniform flavoring. Be especially careful with the red pepper to insure even distribution.

Stuff mixture into cleaned sausage casings, tying ends securely.

Smoke slowly for three to four days.

Refrigerate or freeze.

Prepare links by covering with water, cover kettle, bring to a boil, then let stand (covered) for five minutes.

Other Spices For Sausage

You may wish to experiment by adding some or all of the following to 30 pounds of ground meat:

4 tablespoons garlic salt
3 teaspoons summer savory (ground)
3 teaspoons nutmeg
3 teaspoons marjoram

BRAINS

Cover with water, add 1 teaspoon salt and 2 teaspoons vinegar and soak 1 hour. Remove any loose membranes or other materials. Simmer in salted water for about 30 minutes. Shake dry and chill in cold water.

Prepare a batter of 1 egg and 1 cup water. Dip brain in water, roll in flour or cracker crumbs and fry in cooking oil or other hot fat.

Brains may also be scrambled with eggs.

STEAK AND KIDNEY PIE

1 kidney from most any big game
1 pound venison steak (or other big game) cubed
1 large onion, sliced
1 can mixed vegetables
salt and pepper

Soak kidney in salted water for one hour. Remove skin and tubes and other loose membrane material. Cover with water and simmer 30 minutes.

Cut steak and kidney into cubes (less than 1 inch). Brown in cooking oil. Add onion slices last few minutes. Cover with water and simmer for about 30 minutes or until tender. Thicken with flour blended with water.

Place in greased casserole dish; stir in mixed vegetables. Cover with pastry mix (slit top) or baking powder biscuits. Place in medium oven (300°), and bake until pastry is brown or biscuits are done.

To make the meat go farther, add a second can of mixed vegetables.

TRIPE SOUP

1/2 pound tripe
3 cups cream of celery soup
1/4 cup chopped celery
1/2 cup chopped green pepper

1 teaspoon pepper
1/2 teaspoon salt
1 small onion, chopped

Cover tripe with cold water and let stand three hours. Scrub clean. Simmer in salted water another three hours. Drain and dice (fine).

Sauté onion, celery and green pepper in butter until tender (but not brown). Add all other ingredients, using a suitable pot. Simmer about 40 minutes.

Because of the amount of pepper this will be quite a spicy soup. If it is too hot, reduce pepper to taste.

KIDNEYS IN TOMATO SAUCE

Remove skin, tissue and fat from 2 or 3 wild game kidneys. Discard the core. Slice thin.

Prepare a sauce from the following ingredients:
1 onion, chopped
1 teaspoon salt (level)
1 #2 can tomato sauce
1 cup sliced mushrooms

Sauté the onions in a little butter or oil until clear (also the mushrooms if they are uncooked). Add the other ingredients and cook over low heat for 15 minutes.

While the sauce is cooking, fry the sliced kidneys in butter for about 3 to 5 minutes (depending on thickness of slices).

Using a large skillet (preferably cast iron), cover the kidney slices with 2 cans mixed vegetables, 1/2 teaspoon pepper, 1/2 cup white wine, 1 tablespoon salt and 1 tablespoon parsley flakes. Cook until it starts to boil and then add the sauce. Stir together and continue to cook a few more minutes or until the kidney slices are tender.

Serve over rice.

JERKY

Here's an entirely different taste treat from your big game animals. Jerky makes a great snack and is also ideal for taking along on those outdoor excursions when you want something light but nutritious. Indians, Eskimos and early white settlers used jerky extensively as a way of preserving meat.

The procedure for making jerky is simple, but it takes time:

Use only lean meat—trim away *all* the fat—and cut, with the grain—into strips one-half inch thick and one inch wide. They may be of any length.

Mix together the following for each pound of meat strips:

2 tablespoons salt
1/4 teaspoon cayenne pepper
1/2 teaspoon black pepper
1 tablespoon sugar (preferably brown or maple)

If you like the flavor of garlic, add ½ teaspoon garlic salt.

Lay strips in a baking dish (glass or pottery—not metal), sprinkling the salt-pepper-sugar mixture generously over *each* layer.

Refrigerate for 1 day.

Dry each strip with paper towel and place on over rack—with sides *not touching* or suspend each piece from the rack by running a toothpick through one end. Use a low oven, about 150°, for 5 or 6 hours or until the meat is very dark in color—but not powdery or brittle.

Jerky may be stored in a cool, dry place without refrigeration.

Jerky may be broken into pieces and added to vegetables for a quick stew.

PEMMICAN

Although the exact origin of pemmican is unknown, the plains Indians of this part of the continent are more closely associated with the product than any other group of Native Americans. They literally manufactured tons of the commodity every year for centuries. Not only did it nourish them in travel but it sustained life itself in times of famine. White man quickly learned its value and pemmican became a major trade item by the late 1700's. Although pemmican was made from all kinds of big game animals and even fish, buffalo was the favorite and in the early 1800's Pembina, North Dakota, became the marketing center. Arctic explorers, including Perry and Byrd, used the product extensively and reported that even though their men did not relish it at first they came to find it very satisfying and even looked forward to the next meal. As late as World War I it served as a survival ration and there was even some experimentation during the Second World War.

It is believed the original Indian pemmican contained only powdered or finely chopped dried meat saturated in melted animal fat and stored in airtight animal skins. It was not uncommon to store pemmican for as long as five years. It is said that bone marrow was preferred to other fats. Few whites ever cultivated a taste for the commodity until flavor was added in the form of dried wild fruits and berries. As the trade reached its peak in the early 1800's, fillers and flavoring were added, including oatmeal, potato flour, dehydrated vegetables and a variety of seasonings.

If you want to give it a try, here's one proven recipe:

• Cut about 4 pounds of lean meat from most any big game animal into strips about one-half inch thick and one inch wide. Dry the meat slowly in a low oven, start at 150° for about 5 hours, then lower the temperature to 120° and continue the drying process for another two hours or until the meat can be easily broken or ground into small pieces. Do not let it burn. Indians hung the strips near a fire on the side away from the smoke.

• Cut the dried strips into very small pieces.

• Select one-half pound dried berries or fruit; blueberries work well and may be dehydrated in a low oven. Grind or pound the dried berries until they are "powdery".

• Mix the dried fruit and meat thoroughly.

• Weigh the combined fruit and meat. Stuff the mixture loosely into a large sausage casing (available at most butcher shops) or heavy plastic bags.

• Melt an equal amount of lard or rendered animal fat or bone marrow.

• Pour the hot fat into the casing allowing it to flow through the mixture to the bottom by gravity. *If you use a plastic container, let the fat cool off* but pour before it becomes a solid. Seal out air by tying the ends tightly with heavy string or "baggie" ties. You may have fat left over, depending on how loosely you stuffed the casing with the meat and fruit mixture. You will develop your own taste as to how much fat you wish to use and can adjust accordingly the next time you make pemmican.

• Pemmican may be stored in a cool, dry place without refrigeration.

Next time, experiment with other fruits and/or nuts. Ingredients used in granola make excellent filler; such as whole oats, wheat germ, coconut, sesame seed or sunflower seeds. If you like a sweet flavor, add honey.

A stew may be made by adding pieces of pemmican to a can of mixed vegetables or to dehydrated vegetables and water.

RENDERING ANIMAL FAT INTO LARD

The fat should be rendered just as soon as possible after butchering. The longer you wait, the poorer quality the lard.

Trim the fat from the back of the animal. Other fats may be

used but back fat is best. Trim away *all* lean meat. Chop into cubes about 1/2 inch square or slightly larger.

Use a stainless steel, aluminum or rust-free iron kettle.

The heat required will vary with the animal from about 250 to 400 degrees. Use as much heat as you can without causing the lard to smoke. Stir frequently with a large wooden spoon or paddle. When the cracklings become yellow in color and no more moisture is seen rising from the lard, remove from fire and draw off the liquid into a clean container and place in a cool place. When the substance takes on a creamy texture, stir thoroughly and then refrigerate.

chapter IV

MORE FROM YOUR GAME BIRDS

Game birds are a gourmet food and down through the ages have been considered "fit for a king's table". Tragically, many believe all birds are supposed to taste like chicken or turkey and judge them accordingly. Instead, we should expect a whole new taste, and enjoy it. Because the birds do not come from the meat market, they do require a little more work, but the results are well worth the extra effort.

CLEANING AND PRESERVING GAME BIRDS

The care your birds receive in the hours immediately following the hunt are extremely important in determining their table quality. In fact, on a warm day it is wise to field dress the birds at the time they are shot—do not wait until after shooting hours or until you get home. It is true that ducks and geese may be hung by their necks for several days to make them more tender, but *not in hot weather*.

It takes just a few minutes to "gut out" a bird in the field. For a thorough and quick job without getting your hands dirty -

1) Cut the wind pipe and esophagus in the neck. You can feel them easily with your fingers.

2) Use a piece of stiff wire with a hook bent into one end or a forked stick. Simply insert it into a cut in the rear of the bird and pull out the entrails.

Upland game, such as pheasants and partridges, are easily skinned, but you lose a great deal of flavor when you lose the skin and it is more difficult to keep the meat moist. Pheasants can be easily dry-picked or the feathers may be loosened by submerging the bird into very hot water. On the other hand,

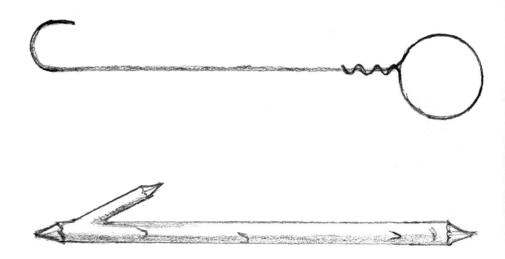

partridges cannot be easily plucked without tearing the skin, but if you have the time, it is worth the effort. You can then prepare them according to your favorite recipe for roast or fried chicken, or try some of the recipes suggested later in this chapter.

Ducks and geese (except for the impossible snow goose) should be plucked, not skinned, if you plan to roast them. Because the snow goose is so hard to pluck, you may as well skin the bird and then roast it under a tent of foil over the breast (so that it will not dry out). A couple of pieces of fat bacon laid on the breast will also help keep the meat moist.

Late season birds may be plucked bare and then "singed" over an open flame to eliminate the down. Earlier in the season, pluck the feathers but leave the down. Submerge the birds briefly (about 10 seconds) in a pail of hot water in which wax has been melted (about half water and half wax). Let the birds lie in cold water or cold air until the wax is thoroughly hardened. The wax and remaining down can then be easily peeled from the carcass using a table knife or spoon. The wax may be saved for future use by again melting it and then straining out the feathers through coarse hardware cloth.

We began this chapter by suggesting that birds be dressed as soon as possible; especially during periods of warm weather. There are many hunters, however, who prefer to hang their ducks, pheasants and geese (always by the neck) for several days before drawing them. The purpose is to make them more tender. This is fine, providing -

- the weather is cool (from just above freezing to 50°F.),
- the birds are not allowed to freeze, thaw out and freeze again, and
- the birds are not badly shot up.

Fowl may be frozen and kept for relatively long periods of time. If you plan to use them in the next month or two, sharp freeze them in heavy foil or a double layer of waxed freezer paper. Be careful to squeeze out as much air as possible to prevent freezer burn. To keep birds for longer periods of time—up to one year—freeze them in water. Half gallon milk cartons make excellent containers for ducks or pheasants.

TRADITIONAL RECIPES
DUCKS
"Quick and Easy" Roast Duck

The first time you try this "fast roast" technique you'll be pleasantly surprised by the rich flavor and juicy meat.

Wash each bird thoroughly inside and out, being careful to remove every trace of lungs, windpipe, etc.

Season with salt and pepper, inside and out.

Stuff with quarters of apples or onions—or most any vegetable you have handy, including potatoes or carrots.

Place birds in roaster or baking dish, breast sides up. Place one or two strips of cheap, fat bacon on each breast.

Add one cup of water (more if you are preparing several birds in a large roaster). Or—use 1/2 cup water and 1/2 cup cooking wine.

Cover roaster and place in preheated very hot oven (450°) for 45 minutes. Uncover for final ten minutes.

Roast Duck - "Easy but not so Quick"

Prepare exactly as above (Quick and Easy) but roast in a 300° oven for two hours or in a slow oven (225°) for three to four hours. Uncover the final half hour to brown birds.

This will be an entirely different flavor than you experienced with the quick, hot oven.

Ducks will be done when the drumstick can be easily "wiggled".

Gourmet Roast Duck with Wild Rice Stuffing and Honey Glaze

Prepare birds by scrubbing inside and out, being careful to trim away scraps of lung, etc.

Place in a large bowl, breasts down and cover with cold water. Add two tablespoons salt per bird. Let stand in refrigerator overnight.

Prepare stuffing:

> 1 cup wild rice, washed (will make three cups cooked rice)
> 1-1/2 cups croutons
> 3/4 cup raisins
> 1/2 cup melted butter or margarine mixed with 1/2 cup
>   hot water
> 1 large onion
> 1/3 pound chopped bologna or summer sausage or polish
>   sausage or luncheon meat

Cook the wild rice according to one of the basic recipes on pages 19-20.

Combine the croutons, raisins, onion and chopped meat. Season lightly with salt and pepper. Try to buy the pre-seasoned croutons, but if these aren't available or if you use dry bread, you may want to add a *little* sage seasoning.

Pour the melted butter-water mixture over the dressing and stir.

Take birds out of salt water, pat dry with paper towel, season with salt and pepper, inside and out.

Stuff the birds loosely (not packed). Additional stuffing may be prepared in foil; the package alongside the bird. If there isn't room in the roaster, just set it in the oven by itself. When prepared separately, the stuffing need not be in as long as the birds—about an hour will do.

Place the birds in roaster breast sides up. Place strip of fat bacon over each breast.

Add about one-half inch of water in bottom of roaster.

Cover and place in preheated low oven (250°). Bake three hours or until tender. Drumsticks should wiggle easily.

Remove cover last half hour. Remove bacon strips and spread coat of honey over breasts to glaze during these last 30 minutes. Orange marmalade also forms a tasty glaze, or baste with orange sauce prepared according to the recipe on page 58.

Duck Gravy

While duck is roasting, cook giblets (heart, gizzard and liver) by simmering in water until tender—about 1 hour.

Chop giblets.

Remove ducks from roaster.

Skim off the excess fat.

Using a spatula, carefully scrape loose the particles from the bottom of the pan. Do not scrape so hard as to loosen severely burned materials.

Using a pint jar with a cover as a shaker, add 1/2 cup water and 1/4 cup flour. Shake well. If a covered jar is not available, use a bowl, add flour and a little water to make a smooth paste. Now add the rest of the water and stir until the mixture is uniform and there are no lumps.

Remove roaster from heat. Add chopped giblets. Slowly stir in the flour and water mixture. Place roaster on low heat on top of stove and allow to simmer, stirring all the while. When the gravy is bubbling all over the roaster, add one tablespoon of Kitchen Bouquet and salt and pepper. Continue to stir over heat for another five minutes and serve. For thicker gravy, add more flour and water mixture.

Scoop dressing from birds and place in serving bowl along with any additional stuffing you may have prepared separately. Ladle a few spoons of juices (or gravy) over the stuffing before serving.

Duck, Goose or Wild Turkey in a Brown Paper Bag

If you find yourself without a roaster or covered baking dish in camp, just use a large, brown paper grocery bag. Once you have tried it, you may like it as well as a conventional roaster, and there is less clean-up mess.

Prepare the ducks as you would for roasting in a pan; stuff them if you wish.

The bag should be large enough so that the ducks do not touch the sides.

The bag should rest on a shallow tray or pan.

For a gourmet touch, fill an oven-proof cup or dish with consumé or onion soup and place this in the bag alongside the ducks. If you are a wine buff, use a cup of your favorite cooking wine.

Close end of bag tightly—paper clips work well.

Roast for two hours.

The drippings that may work through the bag onto the tray— plus those that may be poured from the bag when roasting is done—may be used for making gravy.

The paper bag technique may also be used for GEESE and TURKEYS. Recommended roasting time for these larger birds is as follows:

6 to 8 pound bird - 2-1/2 to 3 hours
8 to 12 pound bird - 3 to 3-1/2 hours

12 to 16 pound bird - 3 to 3-3/4 hours
16 to 20 pound bird - 3-3/4 to 4-1/2 hours
20 to 24 pound bird - 4-1/2 to 5-1/2 hours

Duck Sandwiches

Leftover duck (cold or warmed over) on dark bread with a light coat of mayonnaise is just about the greatest sandwich you'll ever enjoy.

Orange Sauce

Traditionally, duck is served with orange sauce.

2-1/2 tablespoons white sugar
1 cup brown sugar
1 tablespoon grated orange
1 cup orange juice (can be made from Tang or other powdered drink)
1 tablespoon cornstarch

Combine the above ingredients and thicken in sauce pan over medium-high heat; stir to prevent burning. For added zest, stir in a drop of Tabasco sauce.

Use about 1/3 of the sauce to baste the bird during the last 1/2 hour of baking. Pour the balance of the orange sauce over the breasts just before serving.

GEESE

Any duck recipe is appropriate for geese; it just takes considerably longer to get done—depending on the size of the bird (see schedule above).

Because geese are usually fatter than ducks, you may need to pour off or skim off the accumulated grease several times while roasting. Note fat duck treatment on page 62.

Wild rice stuffing (page 22) or the baked fish stuffing (page 91) are both excellent with geese. Traditional sauerkraut stuffing also works well. Use a jar of kraut from your grocer's shelf. One pint will stuff two ducks or a large goose.

PARTRIDGE, PHEASANT, SHARPTAILS, ETC.
Fried

Dissect the bird (with game shears or a knife) into its several parts: drumsticks, thighs, wings and two half-breasts (you may want to cut pheasant breast into four parts). Clean and dry.

Season each piece with salt and pepper.

Roll in flour.

Fry in covered pan over medium heat. Use a generous portion of cooking oil (about 1/3 inch). Turn each piece as it browns. Remove cover after fifteen minutes if you like crisp pieces. Larger pieces take longer. Usually, the meat will be done when all sides are brown, but check larger pieces with fork or knife to be sure. If you are doing several birds, keep pieces warm in a "low" oven.

Mushroom Casserole

Dissect the bird as for frying.

Salt and pepper each piece.

Roll in flour.

Brown each piece in cooking oil or margarine over medium heat.

Place in a casserole or baking dish and cover with mushroom soup. (Add one can of water for each can of soup) If you are a mushroom fancier, add a can of parts and pieces.

Place in preheated 300° over for an hour and a half.

Your wild birds will never be dry or tough.

Wild Rice - Partridge, Sharptail or Pheasant Casserole

See page 21 in chapter II.

Pheasant in Sour Cream

2 pheasants, cut into sections
1 small onion, diced
2 stalks celery, diced
2 cups sour cream
1/2 cup flour
2 T salt
1/2 T pepper

Dissect the birds including cutting the breasts of each bird into four pieces. Mix seasoning into flour and roll each piece therein. Brown slowly in frying pan. Sauté onions and celery pieces. Place pheasant in casserole. Mix onion and celery into sour cream and pour mixture over meat. Cover and bake in 325° oven for 1½ to 2 hours or until tender.

Sharptail Pie

2 sharptails or 1 pheasant or 3 partridges, deboned and cut into bite-size pieces.

1 large onion
2 cans mixed vegetables
1 package baking powder biscuits from the dairy case or
   prepared from scratch
2 whole allspice
4 whole peppercorns
1/2 cup flour
salt, pepper and paprika

Roll the bite-size pieces of bird in seasoned flour and fry slow-ly over low heat until brown. Chop the onion and add to the fry-ing pan about halfway through the frying process. Add 1½ cups of water plus the allspice and peppercorns; cover and simmer until tender. Remove meat from the pan and add 3 cups milk or chicken broth (or soup). Thicken with flour dissolved in water, stirring constantly. Add salt and pepper to taste. Place the meat plus the two cans of mixed vegetables—drained—into a greased casserole. Cover with gravy. Place the baking powder biscuits on top of the mixture, sides touching. Bake at 400° until biscuits are done.

Fried Duck

Early season ducks are often so "pin-feathery" they are best skinned and fried. Skin and debone the breasts. Skin the wings and legs but leave the meat on the bone. Season lightly and roll in flour or cracker crumbs. Fry over low heat.

For a slightly different treatment, cut the breast meat into strips about 1/2 inch square—the length of the breast. Roll in cracker crumbs and fry over low heat—along with the wings and legs.

TOUGH BIRD TREATMENT

There is no sure "rule of thumb" for predicting which birds are old and tough, but it is usually safe to assume that unusually large birds will probably not be very tender. Pinfeathers on ducks late in the season, on the other hand, would indicate younger birds. Young cock pheasants have gray legs and the last of the long wingfeathers will be pointed—not rounded.

The following recipes are guaranteed to not only tenderize tough old birds, but will make them very much fit for the table. They will also be helpful in preparing birds which have been left too long in the freezer.

Parboiled Ducks

Tough old ducks and less tasty species—including golden eyes and rice hens—will be made both tasty and tender by this technique.

Let ducks stand in salted water overnight, breasts down (refrigerated).

Place birds in kettle, breats down, cover with salted water. Bring to a boil; remove after about five to ten minutes of boiling. If you have reason to believe birds are tough, leave a little longer.

Remove ducks from kettle, wash off any grease residue, salt and pepper inside and out.

Place ducks in roaster, breast up, with a strip of fat bacon over each breast.

Place in preheated 250° oven and bake for another three hours. Remove cover last half hour to brown. Orange sauce (page 58), orange marmalade or honey glaze may be added at this time (remove bacon).

This technique is guaranteed to tenderize even the toughest old Greenhead!

Baked with Onion Soup Mix

Fillet the ducks or pheasants and skin.

Do *not* season.

Lay pieces on foil in a single layer.

Place a generous pat of butter or margarine on each piece (about 1/4 pound per bird).

Pour the dry onion soup mix over the meat pieces (one envelope for two ducks or one pheasant).

Fold the foil over the ducks and seal on top.

Place in preheated 300° oven, sealed side up, for an hour and 15 minutes.

The soup mix liquid may be used as a gravy. Simply pour in bowl and add an equal amount of hot water.

Ducks, geese or pheasants you have had in the freezer for a long time are also ideal candidates for this recipe.

The Crockpot Treatment

    2 ducks or 1 small goose
    1/2 cup cooking wine
    2 small apples, quartered

Soak the birds in salt water overnight. Dry and season inside and out with salt and pepper. Stuff with apple sections. Place

1/2 cup cooking wine and 1/2 cup water in bottom of crockpot. Place birds in pot breasts up. Cover and cook 1 hour on high—4 hours on low—and finish on high until leg moves easily. Baste breasts with wine occasionally during last hour. For crisp skin, place under broiler a few minutes—watch carefully so it does not burn.

Barbeque Sauce With Crockpot Ducks or Geese

Use the above recipe but use no wine; use 1 cup water in bottom of pot instead. When bird is tender, quarter with game shears and lay pieces on grill. Baste with your favorite barbeque sauce and cook until sauce shows signs of drying. Turn and baste other side. Five minutes on each side should be adequate inasmuch as the birds are already cooked.

Even those who do not care for ducks or geese will probably enjoy this treatment.

Fat Ducks

Late season ducks are often so fat the meat tastes "greasy" and the stuffing becomes saturated. This can be overcome by standing the ducks in an iron kettle, bottoms down and necks up. Place in a very hot oven (450°) for 30-35 minutes. Throw away the grease and then stuff and roast the ducks via your favorite recipe.

MEAT EXTENDER RECIPES

A single pheasant, duck or partridge can be stretched to satisfy a family of four or leftover portions can be extended for a second meal.

Wild Rice and Partridge, Duck or Pheasant Casserole

    1 cup wild rice (washed)
    flour
    1 partridge, duck or pheasant—deboned and
      cut up into pieces
    1 large onion, chopped
    1 green pepper, chopped
    1 small jar pimentos
    1 can mushroom soup
    1 can water
    salt and pepper

Prepare the wild rice by any of the basic recipes found in Chapter II.

Cut the bird into bite-size pieces, removing all bones. Season, roll in flour and fry in oil slowly over low heat until browned but not "crusty". When it is about done, add the chopped onion, green pepper and celery. Continue frying for another three or four minutes. Add pimento, soup and water.

Place in a greased casserole. Cover and bake in a 300° oven for 1½ hours. Add water while baking to prevent dryness.

If duck is used, cook it first in a crock-pot or very slow oven until the meat can be easily stripped away from the bones.

Partridge Stew Over Baking Powder Biscuits

    1 partridge (or pheasant)—deboned and cut into bite-sized pieces
    1 can mixed vegetables, drained
    1 small onion
    1 package baking powder biscuits from the supermarket dairy case or prepared from scratch
    salt and pepper to taste
    2 bay leaves
    4 peppercorns

Brown the partridge pieces slowly over low heat in oil. Add the chopped onion when the meat is nearly done and continue to cook three or four minutes. Thicken with a little flour made into paste so it will not be lumpy. Add bay leaves, peppercorns, and simmer slowly for 1/2 hour. Add vegetables and continue to simmer for another 1/2 hour. Serve over buttered baking powder biscuits.

Save the Giblets!

GRAVY

The heart, liver and gizzard of your game bird will make your gravy taste extra special. Parboil them until tender. Chop quite fine. Add to your favorite gravy. (See page 56 for duck gravy recipe.)

GIBLETS ON TOAST

Use the above gravy recipe but do not chop the giblets quite so fine (leave them about 1/8" to 1/2" square). Serve over crisp toast.

ENJOYING LESS POPULAR GAME BIRDS

By tradition and law, our generation has limited the varieties of game birds which find their way to our tables to a relative few. In contrast, the Indian and the early settler ate most any bird large enough to make the effort to prepare worthwhile. Many pioneers brought with them from their European homelands the custom of eating even songbirds and sparrows! Today, there are some birds which hunters may legally take that are often overlooked but which could provide some mighty good eating—such as the coot (rice hen, *not* mud hen) and snipe. Even mergansers (fish ducks) can be made quite palatable—along with late season golden eyes and other diving ducks which sometimes turn to minnows for food and therefore taste "fishy" just before freeze-up.

Duck in an Iron Kettle

If you have the time, always let ducks or geese soak in salted water overnight—under refrigeration.

Cut birds in half, lengthwise—with poultry shears or heavy knife.

Clean. Season birds with salt and pepper.

Roll birds in flour and fry in heavily greased frying pan—about 1/3 inch oil—until well browned.

Place ducks in an iron kettle—anyway you can get them in—but remember, it is the breasts that you will want covered with liquid.

Fill kettle with water, covering ducks as much as possible.

For four ducks, add:

> 2 tablespoons allspice
> 2 tablespoons poultry seasoning
> 2 bay leaves
> 10 or 12 whole black peppers

Cover kettle (foil will do) and place in preheated 250° oven or over low-medium heat on top of stove. Let simmer for three hours or until birds are tender.

If the birds are unusually fat, use the technique described on page 62 to get rid of excess fat, before cooking.

Parboiled Ducks

Mergansers, golden eyes and other late season or strong-tasting ducks can be helped a great deal by parboiling as described on page 61.

The "BAKED IN ONION SOUP MIX" recipe also found on page 61, works very well with any stronger tasting varieties.

Coots (Rice Hens)

Coots (not to be confused with mud hens) make excellent eating and are often overlooked by many hunters. Their favorite foods are the same as mallards and other puddle ducks. They have been appropriately called "the partridge of the ricebed".

    4 coots—quartered
    1 large onion, diced
    1 garlic clove
    2 bay leaves
    3 whole allspice
    4 peppercorns

Dredge the pieces of rice hen in seasoned flour and brown, slowly, in butter or cooking oil. Shortly after the browning process begins, add the diced onions and chopped garlic clove. Add enough water to cover meat, add spices and simmer over very low heat for three hours, adding water as necessary.

Coot breasts and legs are also excellent fried. Just skin, roll in cracker crumbs and fry slowly in cooking oil.

Jacksnipes, Rails and Woodcocks

These little birds are mighty tasty and may be prepared with ducks. Because they are so much smaller, you can add them to the roaster when the ducks are about half-done. (Be sure they may be legally taken in your area.)

Woodcocks also migrate in the fall and make excellent eating. They are tasty when prepared by any of the partridge or pheasant recipes. Casserole dishes are an especially effective treatment.

chapter V

MORE FROM YOUR FISH

THE CARE, CLEANING AND PRESERVING OF FRESHWATER FISH

The quality of fish can deteriorate quite rapidly, so for maximum enjoyment—take proper care of your fish just as soon as each is caught (or bought). Here are some basic but important suggestions:

- A live box, live basket or stringer are all fine for keeping fish in good condition—*but only as long as the fish stay healthy*; never tow dead fish around the lake or leave them floating belly-up in your live box. If you use a stringer, the steel-snap variety is excellent for walleyes and bass. Push the steel through both the upper and lower jaws to prevent drowning. Northerns or muskies will twist a steel snap open, so use a nylon rope-type stringer for them—again pushing the steel tip through both jaws. Never string a fish through the gills. A live basket is excellent for panfish.

  The best method is to carry a cooler of crushed ice and throw your fish in as you catch them.

- Even fish that are still alive but are in the process of dying are diminishing in quality.

- Fish fillets may be frozen in ice and kept for several months. Half-gallon milk cartons are ideal.

- Fillets or whole fish may be glazed with ice and kept for several weeks or as long as the ice seals in the quality. Air is the enemy; it dries out the fish and changes the flavor. For proper glazing—chill the fish; then submerge in ice water (with ice chunks or shavings floating in the water) then place them in the coldest part of your freezer. The more rapidly foods are frozen, the better. Repeat the process two or three times for a good glaze.

- Fillets or whole fish may be wrapped in foil or "freezer-wrap" and quick frozen for short periods of time (several weeks).

- Oily fish such as trout or whitefish do not keep well but quality may be substantially restored after thawing by soaking the fillets in milk for two or three hours.

- Smoked fish must be refrigerated for safe keeping. Freezing is not recommended but smoked fish may be frozen if you have too large a supply to consume over a couple of weeks. Frozen smoked fish should be thawed slowly—in the refrigerator.

- Frozen fish keep best at a constant temperature.

Fish cleaning techniques are important, both in terms of quality and reducing waste. Here are some practical suggestions:

- Choose your knife carefully; the blade should be relatively long (about 6 or 7 inches), narrow and *slightly* flexible.

- To get the most possible meat, start your cut as near the gill covers as you can and finish the cut at the very tail itself. Slide the knife along the backbone so as not to waste any of the fish.

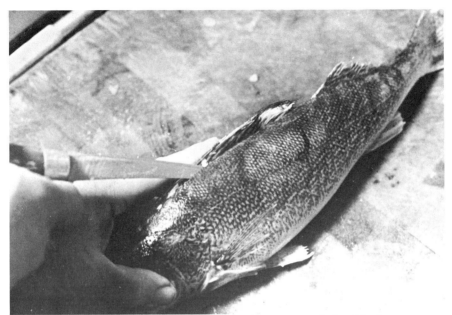

Begin the operation by inserting the point of the blade immediately in back of the head and slightly off center so as to just miss the backbone.

Follow the backbone towards the tail—cutting about halfway through the fish and going all the way through the body after you reach the vent-hole.

Now make a vertical cut along the head, from top to bottom, following close to the gill cover.

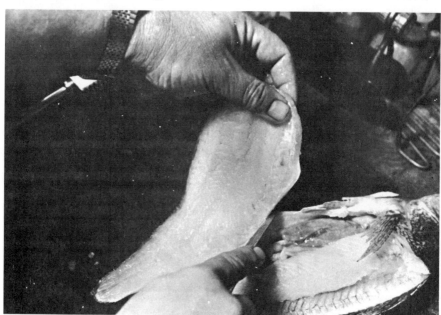

Grasp the loosened fillet at the head-end with your hand that is not holding the knife; as you pull the fillet away from the body, cut with the knife as necessary. Repeat the procedure on the other side of the fish. Now you should have both fillets free from the skeleton.

If you happened to cut through the ribs in the process (some prefer to follow around the ribs), remove the rib cage from the fillet with the tip of your knife.

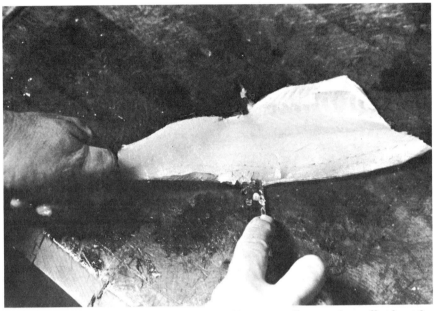

Remove the skin by laying the fillet on a flat surface flesh side up—and then, starting at the tail end, separate the skin from the meat by sliding the knife flat against the skin and moving towards the head-end of the fillet, holding the tail-end of the skin with your fingers or a pliers and pulling on the skin as you push on the knife. It helps to pull the skin from one side to the other as you move the knife forward. Although the knife blade should be held flat, it will help if the cutting edge is slanted against the skin so as not to lose any meat.

You may want to leave the fillets attached to the tail and then use the tail as a handle in the skinning process.

- If you clean the fish in camp and plan to take them home later, do not wash the fillets, just dry them with a paper towel.
- Bass and northerns from warm or muddy waters may have a strong taste in the belly meat. If you suspect this may be the case, trim away that portion of the fillet.

Deboning Northern Pike Fillets

- Northern pike fillets may be deboned (completely). You will have to waste some meat—but it's well worth it. The process works best on fish over three pounds, but with practice you will be able to perform the "surgery" on smaller northerns.

  Fillet the northern the same as you would a walleye or any other fish. Leave the skin on the fillet until after you have finished the deboning process.

  The ridge of meat containing the bones will be visible.

Cut an "inverted V" along the sides of this ridge, but not all the way through the fillet

Make a horizontal cut between the ends of the "V" at the large end of the fillet.

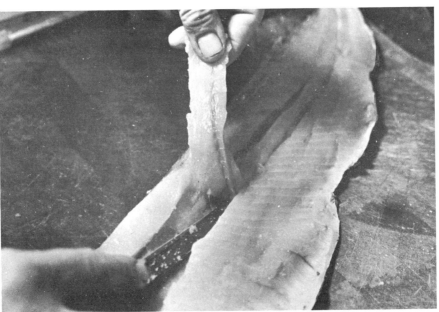

Lift the ridge of bones in one strip out of the fillet as you release it with your knife.

Run your finger (carefully) down the cut; if you feel any "Y" bones left—remove them.

Skin the fillet.

Smaller northerns may be deboned—quickly—by cutting off the tail piece (about 1/4 of the fillet) which usually has few bones. Then make your "V cuts" all the way through the fillet. With this process it is better to remove the skin before you make the cuts just described. You will end up with two rather long, narrow fillets or "fish sticks", plus the tail piece.

- If the fillets from a large fish are too thick to fry well (especially if you like your fish crisp), try slicing the fillet in two—lengthwise, with a horizontal cut.

STANDARD RECIPES

Fried Fish

Without a doubt, most people prefer their fish fried—at least most of the time. Perhaps no other technique brings out so much flavor. Here are some time-proven variations:

Basic Frying

This simple recipe is just about the best we have found for any "good eating" fillet. This includes walleye, northern pike, bass (from clear, northern waters), trout, sunfish, crappies, perch, eelpout, etc. Panfish may be filleted or fried whole.

You may roll your fillets in corn meal, flour, bread crumbs, dry cereal crumbs or special preparations off your grocer's shelf—BUT *cracker crumbs are best.* Cracker crumbs do not detract from the flavor nor are they flavorless; they have just enough saltiness to enhance the taste.

Wash and dry the fillets (paper towels work well). If the fish are large, cut the fillets into pieces about six inches long or less so that they can be easily handled in the pan. If the fish is enormous, cut cross-section steaks about three-fourths of an inch thick.

Prepare the crumbs from ordinary soda crackers. Crush them fine—but not powdery. One-fourth pound of crackers will make enough crumbs for at least one pound of fillets. Place the crumbs in a bowl.

Beat an egg into a cup of water.[1] For more than one pound of fillets, use more eggs and more water (about one egg and one

---

[1]Some prefer milk, but burned milk has a scorched taste.

cup per pound).

Preheat the griddle or frying pan over a medium-hot stove (more hot than medium). Use a generous covering of cooking oil (or butter, margarine or bacon grease)—about 1/4 inch. Add oil as it disappears. A couple of drops of water will spit and spatter when the griddle is ready—but don't burn yourself!

Season both sides of the fillets with salt and pepper. You can be fairly generous with the seasoning because much of it will wash off in the next step, and that is: dip the fillets in the egg and milk mixture. Now dip the fillets in the cracker crumbs, making sure both sides are well covered. Lay the fillets in the preheated frying pan or on the hot griddle.

Fish will cook quickly; the fillets will be done when both sides are a deep brown—about seven or eight minutes on a side (depending on the heat).

When preparing large quantities of fish, fried fillets may be kept warm in the oven until all the fillets are ready. Fry the thick fillets first. Store them in a low oven (200°).

If you are using a frying pan, you can make sure your thick fillets are fully done by adding a couple of spoons of water and covering the pan for a minute or two. This process tends to take away the crispness, so continue to fry fish a couple of minutes on each side after you remove the cover.

In summary, for 2 lbs. of fillets you will need:

one-third lb. cracker crumbs
cooking oil or 1/2 lb. butter or margarine. (Use less heat
   with butter or margarine; just keep it bubbling.)
salt and pepper
2 eggs stirred into 2 cups of water

Serve your fried fish with tartar sauce and/or lemon wedges.

Frying Panfish (sunfish and crappies)

Large sunfish and crappies may be filleted and prepared by the foregoing recipe; however, average size and smaller panfish are more easily fried whole.

Scale the fish; remove head, tail and fins; and draw.

Season the fish inside and out with salt and pepper (use lemon-pepper if available).

Dip the whole fish in a batter of water and eggs (1 egg to 1 cup of water).

Roll the fish in cracker crumbs or corn meal or bread crumbs. (If you prefer flour, batter is not necessary.)

Fry on both sides in a generous portion of oil until brown. For larger fish, cover the pan after you turn the fish and add a few drops of water to steam-cook the fish. Then remove the cover and brown for a crisper skin.

If you prefer to fry your fish in butter, use low heat and cook considerably longer until it flakes easily. Do not let the butter burn—keep it bubbling.

Trout Amandine

A restaurant favorite; here's how they do it:

> 4 trout fillets
> Flour and salt
> 1/2 cup butter
> 1/2 tsp. onion juice
> 1/4 cup blanched, finely slivered almonds
> 1 tablespoon lemon juice

Wash and dry the fish. Dust with salt and flour. Heat half the butter and onion juice in a heavy skillet and cook fish until lightly browned. Remove and place on a hot serving dish. Pour off the grease remaining in the pan and add the rest of the butter. Add the almonds and brown slowly, then add lemon juice and when it foams, pour it over the fish.

BAKED FISH

MINNESOTA BAKED MUSKIE WITH RAISIN STUFFING

This recipe also works well with northern pike or whitefish. On the other hand, all fish are not good baked; even the tasty walleye or the flavorful bass are only fair unless they receive special treatment and seasonings.

Northerns or muskies should weigh five pounds or more, whitefish at least three.

Preparing the fish: Scale and gut the fish; remove the head, tail and all fins. Wash and dry the fish, inside and out.

Score the back of the fish with cross-section cuts about three inches apart—down to the backbone.

Salt and pepper, inside and out and in the cuts.

Preparing the stuffing:

> 1 cup raisins
> 1/4 lb. butter (added to one cup hot water)
> 2 cups croutons or dry bread crumbs
> 1 large onion, chopped but not too fine.
> salt and pepper
> 1 cup chopped bologna (or wieners or polish sausage or luncheon meat)

Place the croutons, raisins, meat and onions in a bowl. Salt and pepper lightly while stirring the ingredients together.

Add and stir in the butter-hot water mixture just before stuffing the fish.

Lay a sheet of foil on the bottom of the roaster.

Stuff the fish (loosely) and place upright on the sheet of foil. Fold the foil up along both sides of the fish—do not cover the back. The foil will hold in the stuffing. If your fish is too long for the roaster, you may cut it in two and bake the two sections side by side.

Leftover stuffing or additional stuffing may be baked in a foil package alongside the fish or even outside the roaster.

Place a strip of bacon and a slice of onion, alternately, over each score (or cut).

Cover the roaster and place in a preheated, 300° oven. After one hour, remove cover and continue to bake until the meat becomes flaky and separates from the backbone (as viewed from the end of the fish). This should take about another half-hour, depending on the size of the fish.

Transfer the baked fish to a platter. Cut through the backbone at each score mark, separating the fish into serving-size portions. The stuffing may be lifted out with each portion as it is served.

Serve with tartar sauce and/or lemon.

LEMON RUBBED AND WINE-BASTED BAKED FISH WITH WILD RICE DRESSING

Choose a large northern pike, muskie, salmon, lake trout or whitefish. Scale and draw the fish. Remove head, tail and fins; wash thoroughly inside and out and dry.

Strain the juice of three lemons; salt lightly. Rub the inside and the outside of the fish—thoroughly—with the salted lemon juice. Refrigerate the fish for two or three hours.

Prepare Stuffing:

1 cup wild rice, washed (will make three cups cooked rice)[2]
1/2 cup melted butter or margarine mixed with 1/2 cup hot water
1 large onion, chopped
1/3 pound chopped bologna, summer sausage
or polish sausage or luncheon meat (optional)
1 cup celery, chopped
1 small green pepper (or 1/3 cup)

[2]You may substitute 1 cup raisins for the wild rice and add 1-1/2 cups croutons. You may prefer to use half white and half wild rice.

Cook the wild rice:

>   3 cups of water
>   1 cup wild rice (washed)
>   salt and pepper
>   1/4 lb. melted butter or margarine

Season water with one tablespoon salt and bring to a boil. Add rice and lower the heat so that the water just simmers. Cook—covered—for about 45 minutes or until the kernels are well opened and the rice is tender. Do not overcook.

Pour off any water that has not been absorbed. Add pepper and a little more salt to taste; pour on the melted butter; and fluff with a fork.

Sauté the celery and onions:

Cook slowly in butter or margarine for about three minutes or until the onions are translucent and the celery is light brown. Combine:

The wild rice, onion, celery, chopped meat and green pepper. Season lightly with salt and pepper. Pour 1/2 cup melted butter combined with an equal amount of hot water over the mixture and stir the ingredients together—thoroughly.

Stuff and bake:

Pat the chilled fish dry and stuff loosely. Leftover dressing may be baked separately in foil alongside the fish. Place a sheet of foil in the bottom of a roaster, then place the fish in the roaster (back up). Bring the foil up halfway around the fish to hold in the stuffing. Place in a preheated medium oven (350°).

Melt 1/4 pound of butter and add an equal amount of white wine. Baste fish from time to time with the wine-butter mixture.

Bake until the meat flakes easily from the large end of the fish (about 15 to 20 minutes per pound).

Transfer baked fish to serving platter; garnish with parsley; and serve with lemon wedges.

BAKED FILLETS

Select two pounds of walleye or other freshwater fish fillets. Season with salt and pepper on both sides.

Dip in milk or water and egg batter and coat both sides with bread crumbs.

Place on a well-greased cookie sheet or in a shallow baking dish. Bake in a preheated medium oven (about 325°) for about 40 minutes.

Meanwhile, prepare a solution of:

3 tablespoons lemon or lime juice
3 tablespoons melted butter

Spoon most of the liquid over the fish after it has been in the oven about 5 minutes. About ten minutes later (15 minutes baking time), sprinkle the remainder of the lemon-butter mixture over the fish and shake paprika and parsley flakes over the fillets. Remove and serve after about 40 minutes of baking time or when the fillets flake easily.

BROILING

Broiled Fillets

A great alternative to frying—especially for those who are on grease-free diets. Any variety of fish may be prepared in this way, but whitefish, walleyes and northerns are particularly tasty when broiled.

Wash and dry the fish; lightly season each fillet with salt and pepper.

Lay the fillets on a sheet of foil (to keep your oven clean).

Lay a piece of bacon on and under each fillet (cheap, fat bacon is best).

Place the fillets under the broiler for about ten minutes or less on each side. Be careful when you turn the fillets; they are very delicate. Place the bacon that was on the bottom on top of the fillet, and vice versa. The purpose of the bacon is to keep the fillets from drying out and from sticking to the foil. If you have no bacon on hand, baste with cooking oil, margarine or whatever.

Serve with tartar sauce and/or lemon. It may remind you of lobster—but it is more tender. You may want to try dipping bite-size pieces into drawn butter (seasoned with a little salt and lemon).

Foil-wrapped Fillets

This technique provides an opportunity for a great variety of treatments—everything from a single fillet broiled in butter to a complete meal of fish and vegetables for several people, wrapped in a single package.

Use heavy duty foil—lightly greased.

Individual fillets may be wrapped in foil with a little butter (1/4 stick) and lightly seasoned with salt and pepper. Other seasonings may be substituted or added such as slices of onion, pepper, tomato or combinations thereof. Broil the fillet about 7 or 8 minutes on each side. Actual time will vary with the thickness of the fillet.

A complete meal may be prepared for four in a single package:

    4# fillets (most any kind)
    6 medium, cooked potatoes—sliced (or two #2 cans)
    1 large onion, thickly sliced
    1 small green pepper, sliced
    1/4 pound butter (1 stick)
    1 #2 can tomatoes (pour off juice)
    Salt and pepper

Lightly grease a large piece of heavy duty foil and lay it flat.

Lay two pounds of fillets in the center of the foil; they may overlap slightly. Season lightly with salt and pepper.

Cover the fish with the sliced potatoes, onion, green pepper and tomatoes (without the juice).

Place the remaining two pounds of fillets on top of the vegetables and season lightly.

Bring the foil up over the meal and *seal well* all the way around.

Place on the grill for about 20-25 minutes, turning once.

Serve with hot coffee, bread and a "doctored" large can of baked beans.[3] (Add brown sugar, catsup and a little onion to the beans, stir, and heat. The amount of brown sugar and catsup will depend on your taste, but try 1/3 cup brown sugar and 1/3 cup catsup for a starter.)

BOILING AND POACHING
Poached Fish[4]

Here is a very different and exciting way to prepare firm and oily fish such as lake trout or whitefish.

Fillet the fish, remove the skin and cut into serving-size pieces about six inches long. (The size doesn't really matter; you just want the pieces small enough to handle easily in the container you use for poaching.)

Fill a kettle about two-thirds full with *cold* water. Salt heavily (about one tablespoon per quart). Place the pieces of fish in the *cold* water.

Add two or three bay leaves or any other spices you prefer, such as whole black pepper or whole allspice. Add two tablespoons of vinegar—this helps kill house odors.

---

[3]"Doctor" the beans by adding generous portions of brown sugar and catsup before heating.
[4]Courtesy Edward Morey, Motley, Minnesota.

Bring to a boil—gradually. When the water has attained a "rolling boil", cut the heat back so that the water just simmers. Allow the kettle to simmer for twelve to fifteen minutes or until the fish can be flaked with a fork. Be careful not to overcook; this will make the fish tough.

Remove the poached fish and place on a platter; drain. Flake the fillets with a fork into fairly large pieces (bite-size). Season with salt and pepper and brush the surface of each piece with melted butter.

The fish is now ready for serving, or—you may try stirring the fish, seasoning, and butter together, or instead of brushing the butter on the fish, serve melted butter on the side in a custard bowl or small dish and let your guests dip the fish as you would dip lobster.

Wisconsin Trout Boil

This recipe comes from the shores of Lake Michigan where it is used with all kinds of trout—from "lakers" to "browns".

Prepare about one pound of trout fillets per person.

Vegetables are boiled along with the fish. Use whole potatoes (skins on), carrots, onions or other "root" vegetables.

Use a 12 quart kettle or larger. Special "fish boil kettles" are available in many locations around the Great Lakes. These kettles contain removable baskets which hold the fish and also have vented covers.

Ingredients to serve six:
   4# trout fillets
   6 large potatoes—skins on but washed
   6 medium, sweet onions—peeled
   2 cups salt

Pour 8 quarts of water into the kettle and add potatoes. Cover and bring to a *rolling* boil. Now add the onions and/or other vegetables and 1 cup of salt.

Allow the vegetables to cook for 20 minutes before adding trout.

Place the fish in a dish towel or cheesecloth (unless your kettle comes equipped with a basket). Lower the fish into the water until they are completely submerged but not touching the vegetables on the bottom of the kettle. When the water resumes a *rolling* boil, add the other cup of salt and cover the kettle. If the cover is not vented, leave an opening for the escaping steam.

It is important that you maintain a *rolling boil* at all times or the food will be too salty.

-81-

After 10 or 12 minutes, check the fish for flakiness and the vegetables for softness. When the fish flake easily and the potatoes are readily penetrated with a fork, your meal is done.

Serve with drawn butter flavored with lemon juice and garnished with parsley flakes.

OFTEN OVERLOOKED VARIETIES AND TREATS

Perch

CHEESE-COATED PERCH

Save those larger perch and give them this treatment:
  1 pound fresh perch fillets (or other freshwater fish)
  1/4 cup all purpose flour
  1 beaten egg
  1 tsp. salt
  Dash pepper
  1/4 cup fine dry bread crumbs
  1/4 cup grated Parmesan cheese
  1/4 cup shortening
  1 eight ounce can tomato sauce
  1/2 tsp. sugar
  1/2 tsp. dried basil leaves, crushed

Cut fish into serving size portions. Coat with flour and dip into a mixture of egg, salt and pepper, then dip into a mixture of bread crumbs and cheese. Fry fish slowly in a skillet or hot shortening until browned on one side. Turn and brown other side. Combine tomato sauce, 1/4 cup water, sugar and basil in a saucepan. Simmer 10 minutes and serve with the fish.

PERCH WITH PARSLEY AND DILL

This is a turn-of-the-century favorite:
  8 medium sized perch, dressed (scale and remove heads, tails and fins; and drain.)

Cover bottom of baking dish with 1/4 cup finely chopped parsley and arrange the fish in the baking dish.

Top with:
  2 tablespoons finely chopped parsley
  2 tablespoons chopped fresh dill or
  1 tsp. dill seed

Pour 1/4 cup hot water around the fish. Bake at 350° for 20 to 25 minutes and serve. Whole crappies and sunfish also respond well to this treatment.

PERCH TEMPURA

Ingredients:

    2 lbs. fresh fish fillets, salted to taste
    1 lemon, halved
    1/2 Tempura Batter recipe
    1 qt. vegetable oil

Cut fish fillets into bite-sized pieces and drain well on paper toweling. Season with salt and squeeze lemon juice over the fish.

Tempura Batter

    2 c. sifted flour
    3 egg yolks
    2 c. ice water

Sift the flour 3 times. Combine the egg yolks and water in a large bowl over ice and beat with a whisk until well blended. Add the flour gradually, stirring and turning the mixture from the bottom with a spoon. Do not overmix. The flour should be visible on top of the batter. Keep the batter over ice while dipping and frying.

Spear pieces of fish and dip in the batter, drain slightly and fry in deep fat heated to 360 degrees for about 5 minutes, turning to brown evenly.

Bullheads

BULLHEAD WITH TOMATO SAUCE

Ingredients:

    3 1 lb. bullheads or other fish, dressed.
    1 eight ounce can tomato sauce
    2 tablespoons salad oil
    1 teaspoon cheese-garlic salad dressing mix or Italian
      salad dressing mix
    1/2 tsp. salt
    Grated Parmesan cheese

Place fish in a greased shallow baking pan. Combine tomato sauce, salad oil, dressing mix and salt. Brush inside cavities with sauce, pour remaining sauce over and around fish. Sprinkle with Parmesan cheese. Bake at 350° for about 40 minutes until fish flakes easily. Bullheads are excellent fried.

BAKED-IN-WINE BULLHEADS

    4 medium size bullheads
    2/3 cup white cooking wine
    1 lemon, thinly sliced

Skin bullheads, wash and dry. Season inside and out with salt and pepper. Brush inside and outside of each fish with wine. Place the balance of the wine in the bottom of a baking dish (about 1/2 inch deep). Lay the bullheads in the bottom of the dish—not touching each other. Sprinkle the fish with paprika and then lay the lemon slices on top of the fish. Cover baking dish and bake at 300° for 45 minutes or until tender. Uncover the last 15 minutes.

Carp

SWEET AND SOUR CARP

This one's straight from China! (Collected by the author while visiting the Chinese mainland.)
Ingredients:

    1 fresh fish, bass, walleye, etc. about 3 pounds live
       weight, scaled and dressed.
    cornstarch
    1 1/2 quarts oil
    Sweet and sour sauce (below)

With a sharp knife make 5 or 6 *deep* diagonal slashes on each side of fish. Shake fish so that it opens up. Sprinkle both sides with cornstarch. Heat oil in a large iron kettle or pan to 375° and carefully place fish into oil. You can cut fish in half and fit together after cooking if your kettle is not large enough. Fry 7 to 10 minutes on each side, until deep golden brown turning gently. Carefully remove from kettle and drain well. Place on a large platter and serve with warm sweet and sour sauce.

Sweet and Sour Sauce:

    3/4 cup sugar
    1/2 cup rice wine or cider vinegar
    1/2 cup catsup
    1/2 cup water
    juice of 1 lemon
    1 tsp. soy sauce
    1/4 cup cornstarch dissolved in 1/4 cup water
    1/4 cup frozen baby peas

Combine sugar, vinegar, catsup, water and lemon juice in a saucepan. Cook over medium heat 3 to 4 minutes. Stir in soy sauce and dissolved cornstarch. Bring to boil, stirring constantly. Cook until thick and clear. Stir in the peas and heat for 3 minutes and pour over fish.

STEAMED CARP

Don't turn up your nose 'til you try it! More carp is eaten in this world than any other fish.

    1 3 pound fresh carp
    1 medium onion, sliced
    2 sprigs parsley
    1 bay leaf
    3 whole peppercorns

Pour water into poacher or large skillet to depth of 1/2 inch. Add onion, parsley, bay leaf, peppercorns and salt. Bring to boil. Place carp on a greased rack, set into skillet, cover and cook until it flakes easily (about 20 to 25 minutes). Drain and serve with Horseradish Sauce or Hollandaise Sauce.

Smelt

These little silvery fish from the Great Lakes—that drive normally sane people apparently out of their minds as they drive hundreds of miles and stay up half the night—are worth the effort, providing you eat them fresh. They are an oily fish and the flavor deteriorates rapidly. Keep them on (and in) crushed ice until you get home; then enjoy them immediately. They may be frozen in water and will still be good to eat, but not as delicious as fresh.

SMELT IN BEER BATTER

Smelt may be fried in flour or cracker crumbs, but are probably at their best deep fried in beer batter:

Pour one-half cup of beer into a bowl and let stand overnight or until "flat".

Add the beer and a tablespoon of cooking oil to two cups of white flour. Mix. Beat the whites of three eggs until stiff and work them into the batter. If mixture is too heavy, add a little water.

Dip the dressed smelt into the batter and deep fry in hot cooking oil (about 375°) until golden brown. The batter tends to insulate the fish so make certain they are done before serving.

SMELT IN BARBECUE SAUCE

1 pound fresh smelt

Ingredients:
 1 8 ounce can tomato sauce
 1/2 cup chopped onion
 2 tablespoons brown sugar
 2 tablespoons vinegar
 1 tablespoon Worcestershire sauce
 1 tablespoon water
 2 teaspoons prepared mustard
 1/4 tsp. salt

Clean, rinse and wipe smelt dry. Combine all ingredients, except smelt. Marinate smelt in tomato mixture, cover and refrigerate for several hours. In a large skillet bring smelt and tomato mixture to boiling. Reduce heat and simmer uncovered til fish are done. 8 to 10 minutes. Makes 3 to 4 servings.

Eelpout

EELPOUT HORS D'OEUVRES (mock scallops)

Eelpout (freshwater cousins of the codfish) are actually very good filleted and fried. But because the meat is firmer then walleyes and northerns, they lend themselves very well to this recipe and will remind you of scallops.

Cut the eelpout fillets into bite-size pieces—about the size of scallops.

Season with salt and pepper.

Dip in water-egg batter (1 egg to a cup of water).

Roll in cracker crumbs.

Fry in about 1/4 inch oil, turning until brown on all sides. The crisper the better—but not burned. Serve hot.

Now if you can forget what the fish looks like, get ready to enjoy a real delicacy! If you cannot forget, try walleye or perch tidbits.

Furthermore, there is nothing wrong with eelpout fillets—but don't hide the delicate flavor with heavy batter. People who have not had a look at this poor, ugly creature will choose eelpout over walleye nine times out of ten! Just tell them it's freshwater codfish.

Freshwater Hearing

HERRING SALAD (Swedish Sil Salad)

This is a favorite Smorgasbord item brought to this country

by Scandinavian immigrants in the last century. The following ingredients are for 8 to 10 servings:

1 large salt herring
1 cup cooked beets, diced
1 1/4 cup cooked potatoes, diced
1 cup diced roast beef (or beef or ham)
1 pickle, finely chopped (medium—sweet)
1 1/2 apple, medium, peeled and diced
2 Tablespoons vinegar
1 teaspoons vinegar
1/8 teaspoon white pepper
1 hard boiled egg; cut white into strips, mash yolk
1/4 cup whipping cream (whip) or 1/2 cup sour cream

Soak the herring in water overnight. Rinse, remove skin and bones.

Mix herring, diced beets, diced potatoes, diced meat, diced apple, chopped pickle and add vinegar, sugar and pepper.

Turn out on a platter and garnish with mashed egg yolk in center with egg white strips arranged in a spiral around the yolk. You may also add parsley and small, cooked beets for decoration.

Serve with either whipped or sour cream. Some prefer to stir the cream into the salad before it is placed on the platter.

BOILED FRESHWATER HERRING

Remove heads, tails, fins and entrails—one or two fish per person.

The "true" Scandinavian leaves the heads on for "handles" when removing the backbones!

Place in boiling salted water (1 teaspoon per quart) for about 15 minutes or until the backbone can be pulled *easily* from the meat, leaving delicious flakes and morsels. Season to taste with salt and pepper. Pour melted butter over the fish and fluff with a fork.

Serve with boiled potatoes.

Herring may also be fried. Scale and clean the fish, season, roll in flour, and then fry crisp in fairly deep oil. But there will be a lot of bones.

Early Scandinavian settlers in the Midwest brought with them the custom of broiling herring over an open fire, holding them with tongs.

Sucker

BAKED SUCKER[5]

1 green pepper, chopped	1/2 cup cooking oil
1/4 cup diced celery	4 lbs. sucker
1 carrot, diced	salt and pepper
1 onion, sliced	flour
2 tomatoes, chopped	paprika

Combine vegs. and place in baking dish with oil. Use sucker, whole or sliced; season with salt and pepper, roll in flour, place on vegetables and sprinkle with paprika. Bake uncovered in a 375° oven 40 mins. or until browned. Baste with liquid in pan two or three times. Serve with corn meal muffins, butter and red current jelly.

POTTED SUCKER[5]

1/3 cup cooking oil	5 gingersnaps
2 lbs. sucker, sliced into pieces	1 1/2 cups warm water
2 onions, sliced	1/2 tsp. whole mixed spices
2 carrots, sliced	1/4 tsp. salt

Pour half of oil in baking dish, arrange half of fish on top, cover with half the onions and carrots, adding remaining fish and vegetables. Soften gingersnaps in water and stir until smooth. Add spices and salt and pour over fish. Add remaining oil and water, if necessary to cover fish. Cover dish and bake in slow oven at 325° 45 mins. to an hour. Serves 4.

Sucker is also one of the better fish for smoking.

Fish Livers

Northerns, muskies and eelpout all have large livers; they can easily weigh a quarter pound.

Cut into thin slices, season very lightly with salt and pepper and fry over low heat—preferably in bacon grease. What will it taste like? Liver, of course!

Fish livers are also excellent smoked.

Walleye—But Different

WALLEYE CHEEKS

The cheek meat of a hog is a real delicacy; on the market it is labeled a "pork cutlet". Likewise with the "hogger" walleyes or

[5]Courtesy Mrs. Jerry Fuller, Author: "Fuller's Golden Book of Fish and Game Recipes". To order, write Fuller's Tackle Shop, Park Rapids, MN.

lakers—so save those cheeks; they, too, are a great delicacy when fried along with the fillets. You will find them a little more firm—like scallops.

Additional meat may be salvaged from the head. Indians and Eskimos sometimes take out the eyes, cut the lower jaw in two and then spread out the head and broil it over an open fire. Fish heads are also used as a base for soups in many parts of the world.

WHOLE BABY WALLEYES

Don't despair when a little walleye is too injured to throw back. Scale it, remove head, fins, tail and entrails. Fry as you would a pan fish.

WALLEYE FILLETS WITH SKIN ON

It is no coincidence that fish bought in the market have their scales removed and the skin on. Much of the walleye flavor is in the skin. Walleyes are difficult to scale; but it is worth the effort. Fry according to any of the recipes in this chapter, with the skin side especially crisp.

Roe and Milt

FRIED FISH EGGS

Sunfish and crappie eggs are especially tasty fried. Wash them carefully so as not to break the membrane. Dip them in seasoned flour or season first with salt and pepper and roll in cracker crumbs. Fry slowly in butter over medium heat.

They are delicious served with either white or red tartar sauce.

BOILED AND BROILED ROE (eggs)

1/2 pound fish roe (especially whitefish eggs)
3 tablespoons lemon juice
4 tablespoons melted butter
1 teaspoon salt

Wash the roe carefully so as not to break the membrane. Dry on paper towel. Bring a quart of water to a boil, add the lemon juice and drop the roe into the water. Remove with large slotted spoon after 5 minutes. Drain, brush with the melted butter. Place under a broiler for a few minutes until brown. Serve with bacon or breakfast sausage.

WHITEFISH ROE[6]

Milk the roe from freshly netted whitefish into a clean container.

Rinse in a sieve.

Place in a bowl.

Finely chop one onion for each quart of roe. Gently stir in the onion and add salt and pepper to taste.

Let stand 24 hours under refrigeration.

Serve raw on crackers—a remarkable hors d'oeuvres.

FISH EGGS WITH HEN EGGS

Use sunfish, crappie, perch or whitefish roe and milt. The size of the roe sacks will vary with the type and size of the fish. Use about 1/2 cup of eggs and then add a pair of milt from the male fish for each pair of roe in the cup.

Saute 1/4 cup chopped onion in 1/4 pound butter. You may wish to add a little garlic or other favorite spice. Add the eggs and milt, breaking their sacks and stir them together for a few minutes (using low heat). Meanwhile, beat two chicken eggs. Add to the fish eggs and milt, stirring them together. For added flavor, use a drop of Tabasco sauce or a teaspoon of soy sauce. Scramble and fry until done.

Serve with bacon and toast.

MILT DISHES

Milt, the sperm of the male fish, is a delicacy—particularly from whitefish, salmon, or members of the trout family. Remove the milt when you clean the fish; rinse it well in cold water, and remove the blue vein present with most fish. It is fragile and, therefore, should be handled with care. You may prepare milt with fish, using the same covering (flour or cracker crumbs, for example) or batter. As an hors d'oeuvres it is a delightful conversation piece. You will find it has a mild, rather sweet, non-fishy taste.

Milt also may be baked. Dip it first in milk or water and egg batter and then gently roll in crumbs or flour. Bake in a greased pan or baking dish.

It may even be used in casserole dishes as a fish substitute. Use alternate layers of milt, cracker or bread crumbs, and mixed vegetables. Cover the whole thing with cream of mushroom soup.

Serve fried or baked milt with lemon or your favorite tartar sauce.

[6]Courtesy Joe Skala, Ely, Minnesota

New Ways to Fix Old Favorites

CHARCOAL BAKED WHOLE FISH

For a real outdoor flavor, give this recipe a try.

Dress a large fish, such as a northern pike, muskie, whitefish or lake trout. Walleye is not at its best baked, but this may well be the best of the baking recipes for this delicious fish. Scale the fish (unless it is a lake trout). Cut off the head, tail and fins. When you draw the fish, make a single cut down the center of the stomach so that the body cavity will hold as much stuffing as possible.

Prepare your favorite dressing—or try this one:
    3 cups croutons or dry bread crumbs
    1 large onion, chopped
    1 cup celery, chopped
    1 small can mushrooms, sliced
    1/4 pound (1 stick) margarine or butter, melted
    1/2 cup hot water

If croutons are not seasoned or if you use bread crumbs, season with salt and pepper and 1/2 teaspoon sage and/or poultry seasoning.

Sauté the onion in the butter or margarine; when the onion is translucent (but not brown), add the 1/2 cup hot water. Place the croutons (or bread crumbs) and chopped celery in a bowl. Pour the butter-water-onion mixture over the contents and stir well. Add seasoning—evenly.

Stuff the body cavity and sew up the fish. Extra dressing may be prepared by wrapping it in foil and placing it along side the fish on the grill.

Place the fish on its side on the charcoal grill (over pre-ignited charcoal that has turned gray, thus indicating it is ready). If your grill has a cover, baking should take about 8 minutes per pound. Without a cover it will take about twice as long and you must turn the fish when it is about half done. You may check doneness by using a fork to see if the meat will flake easily around the exposed backbone at the large end of the fish. Baste from time to time with melted butter.

To avoid flames burning the fish, place a piece of foil directly under the fish and bank the charcoal on each side of the foil.

BAKED IN THE CAMPFIRE

Clay is essential to this recipe, but it is probably available more places then you think. It is commonly found in the banks of most rivers and streams or in the lowlands near lakes. If you suspect the soil may contain clay, add a little water and try molding it with your hands.

Use whole, dressed fish rather than fillets. Scale and take off the head, tail and fins. Since it is difficult to envelope a large fish in clay, select smaller walleyes or bass or try crappies or sunfish.

Season the inside of the body cavity with salt and pepper.

Wrap the fish tightly in foil to keep out all dirt.

Moisten the clay until it can be worked with your hands. Mold the clay entirely around the fish—at least 1/2 inch thick.

Place the fish in the coals of the fire for one hour.

Break the clay open; unwrap the foil; split the fish open down the backbone into the two halves.

Serve with potatoes, also roasted in the fire.

GROUND NORTHERN

A real taste delight for fish lovers: a crisp-fried, hamburger size fish patty served on a bun and garnished with tartar sauce, lettuce leaf and a slice of tomato.

If some bones sneak through, put the fillets through the grinder a second time.

Mix one egg into each pound of ground fish so that the patties may be formed more easily and will hold together better.

Fry the patties on both sides until brown—on a well-greased griddle or in a frying pan. If you like the outside of your fish-burgers crisp, try deep-fat frying; use enough oil so that the patty is about half-covered; when one side is done, turn the patty over. Be sure the oil is hot before you fry fish patties or they will absorb grease.

Leftover ground fish may be preserved by freezing.

FISH PATTIES[7]

Five pounds of fish fillets—diced (boneless). Walleye is probably the best but the recipe also works well with bass, northerns, crappies, etc.

2 eggs
1 cup pancake flour or bisquick
1/2 medium onion, chopped very fine
1/4 medium green pepper, chopped fine
3/4 cup milk

Dice the fish into pieces about 1/4 inch "square".

Beat the eggs, then stir them together with the other ingre-

[7]Courtesy Neil Krough, Staples, Minnesota.

dients in a bowl. The mixture should have the consistency of potato salad. If it is too "runny", add flour; if it is too stiff, add milk.

Spoon the mixture onto a hot grill and fry as you would pancakes—turning over.

FLAKED TROUT SANDWICH SPREAD

Poach lake trout (or salmon) until the fish can be easily separated into flakes with a fork.

Mix two parts of flaked fish to one part of mayonnaise (or according to personal preference) and spread on sandwich bread.

Flakes from leftover fried fillets may also be used.

For variety—add finely chopped lettuce, celery and/or green pepper (about 1/4 cup each to each cup of flaked fish). Also—try substituting French dressing for part or all of the mayonnaise.

Microwave Baked Fish

Different brands of microwave ovens require different times and slightly different treatment. Check your own manual before using any of these recipes.

WHOLE TROUT (OR OTHER SMALL FISH)

Dress a one pound trout per person. (Leave on head and tail but gut and wash.) Rub inside and out with lemon wedge; season lightly with salt and pepper. Lay in baking dish and cover head and thinner part with foil (providing foil may be used in your microwave). Cover with plastic; vent a few places with a fork.

About six minutes will cook one trout; add about three minutes for each additional fish.

Garnish with parsley and serve with lemon wedges and/or tartar sauce.

BAKED NORTHERN (OR OTHER LARGE FISH) WITH OYSTER STUFFING

Oyster dressing:
       1 cup chopped (not too fine) oysters
       1 medium onion, chopped
       1/2 cup celery, chopped
       2 cups seasoned croutons or bread pieces
       salt and pepper (using less if croutons are pre-seasoned)
       1 stick butter (1/4#) melted
       3/4 cup hot water

Sauté the chopped onion in the melted butter until translucent (about 3 or 4 minutes over low heat). Mix with other ingredients.

Scale northern and remove head, tail, and fins and draw. Wash thoroughly and rub inside and out with lemon wedge. Season lightly.

Stuff northern and set upright on oven-proof dish.

Brush outside of northern with Kitchen Bouquet and melted butter (in that order).

Cover with plastic (vented) and cook in microwave oven for about 20 minutes (for a northern that weighs 5 or 6#'s before cleaning). If fish does not flake easily, return to oven, estimating time by degree of doneness.

If fish is not brown enough, brush again with Kitchen Bouquet.

Brush with lemon-butter sauce before serving. (1/4# melted butter and 1 tablespoon lemon juice)

Pickled Fish[8]

Step #1: fillet the fish as you would a walleye—don't worry about the bones. Cut fish into small (herring-size) pieces. Wash.

Prepare a brine solution by adding one cup of salt (preferably pickling salt) to four cups of water.

Cover the fish pieces with the brine solution and let stand overnight.

Step #2: wash off the pieces of fish and soak in white vinegar three to four days.

Step #3: drain, rinse and place in jars (pint size is most convenient).

Prepare a pickling solution as follows:

To two cups of vinegar (if you like to use wine in cooking, use one cup of wine and one cup of vinegar) add -
  one chopped onion (not fine)
  one sliced lemon
  2 tablespoons mustard seed (level)
  1 3/4 cup sugar
  4 bay leaves
  5 whole cloves
  1 tablespoon peppercorns (level)
  5 or 6 small red peppers
  1 tablespoon whole allspice

Bring the solution to a boil, then cool and pour over the fish.

Step #4: pour the pickling solution over the fish pieces you

---

[8]Courtesy Mrs. Donald Hester, Cass Lake, Minnesota

have already packed in the jars (fairly tightly). Cover and refrigerate at least three to four days before serving.

Five to six pounds of cleaned and cut-up northerns will yield approximately one gallon of pickled fish.

FISH EXTENDERS AND LEFTOVERS

So you only caught one fish?! No problem.

Scandinavian Fish Soup

> 1 1/2 pounds boneless fish (salmon, walleye, northern, bass, trout, etc.), cut into half-inch cubes.
> 2 cups milk
> 3 cups water
> 1/2 cup celery, chopped
> 1 medium onion, sliced (pick apart the slices)
> 3 large potatoes, diced (bite-size chunks)
> 10 peppercorns
> 1/2 tablespoon salt
> 1/2 stick butter (1/8 pound)
> 1 tablespoon flour

Start with the 3 cups of water in a kettle; add the potatoes and bring to a boil. Add the fish, salt, whole black peppers, onion and celery and continue at a slow boil until potatoes can be easily pierced with a fork.

Mix the tablespoon of flour into the milk until smooth. Reduce heat to "simmer". Add the flour-milk mixture to the soup and stir until thouroughly blended. Add butter and continue heat until butter is melted (about 5 minutes).

Fish Chowder

> 1/2 cup chopped onion
> 1/4 cup chopped green pepper
> 2 tablespoons butter
> 1 10 3/4 ounce can condensed tomato soup
> 1 14 1/2 ounce can evaporated milk
> 1 chicken bouillon cube, crushed
> Dash garlic powder
> 1 pound fresh fish poached and flaked (2 cups)—try bass, northern or walleye.

In a 3 quart saucepan cook onion and green pepper in butter until tender but not brown. Add soup, evaporated milk, bouillon cube and garlic powder. Stir in the cooked fish and heat through.

Salmon Loaf

Ingredients:

> 2 cups flaked salmon (from leftovers or after boiling)
> 2 cups bread crumbs
> salt to taste
> 1 stick melted butter (1/4#)

Mix salmon flakes, bread crumbs and melted butter. Salt lightly as you mix.

Spoon into greased casserole or baking dish—about 2 inches deep. Bake in a medium oven (350°) for about 30 minutes.

Serves four.

Fish Gumbo

Here's a "fish-stretcher" from the Deep South. You will need the following ingredients:

> 1/4 cup butter
> 1/2 cup chopped onion
> 1 medium-sized green pepper, chopped
> 1/2 cup chopped celery
> 1 28 oz. can of tomatoes
> 1 15 1/2 oz. can okra
> 1 cup water
> 1/4 tsp. dried thyme leaves
> 1 teaspoon salt
> 1 lb. fish fillets, cut into bite sized pieces
> 2 cups cooked rice

Melt butter in a large saucepan over moderately low heat. Add onion, green pepper and celery. Cook until tender (about 3 or 4 minutes). Add tomatoes, okra, water, thyme and salt and simmer for 15 minutes, stirring occasionally. Add fish and cook 10 minutes or until fish is easily flaked. Spoon 1/2 cup hot rice into each soup bowl before filling with the fish mixture.

Grilled Fish Sandwiches

Bored with the same old sandwiches? Here's an exciting variation:

> 1 pound any fish, cooked and flaked
> 1/4 cup Thousand Island salad dressing
> 12 slices bread
> 6 slices process Swiss cheese
> 6 tablespoons butter
> 2 tsp. finely chopped onion

Combine flaked fish and dressing, spread on slices of bread. Place one slice of cheese on each and top with remaining bread. Blend butter and onion together. Spread on both sides of sandwiches. Grill until brown and cheese melts. Serve while hot.

Flaked Trout Casserole

Poach 1# of lake trout fillet until the fish can be easily flaked with a fork.

Ingredients to serve 4:

Flaked trout from 1# fillet (a little over 1 cup)
1 can mushroom soup
1 3 oz. pkg. cream cheese
1 tablespoon chopped onion
1 tablespoon table mustard
1/4 cup milk
2 tablespoons pimento
1 cup cooked macaroni
1/2 cup bread crumbs
2 tablespoons melted butter

Soften the cheese and blend into the soup—using a blender or mixer. Stir in the flaked trout, onion, mustard, macaroni, milk and pimento.

Pour mixture into a casserole. Mix crumbs and melted butter and sprinkle on top.

Bake in medium oven (350°) for 25 minutes.

Smoked Fish in Wine

1 pound smoked fish
1 cup your favorite wine

Marinate the smoked fish (bite-size pieces) in the wine for one hour. Serve on crackers.

Fish Heads

As indicated earlier in this chapter, there is a good deal of meat on the fish head. The cheeks fry up very well and are firm, like scallops. Indians, Eskimos and early white settlers frequently broiled the heads over coals, after taking out the eyes and gills. Slit the lower jaw, then flatten the head out with the palm of your hand, season and broil.

Another favorite, even in Europe, is to use the head (minus the eyes and gills) as a base for fish soup. Whatever is left after you fillet a fish may also be used. Simply simmer the heads and scraps in seasoned water for about an hour. Remove the loose bones and the skeleton of the head (just flake the meat off into the broth).

To one quart of broth, add:

    1 cup chopped onion
    1 cup chopped celery
    2 potatoes, diced
    3 thick slices bacon, chopped or 1/2 cup diced ham

After the vegetables are tender, add 1 can whole kernel corn and continue to heat for another 10 minutes.

Serve with a large pat of butter in each bowl.

Freshwater Clam Chowder

Use a short, dull, heavy-bladed knife to pry open the shells. Cut the muscle away from the shell. Discard the neck and jelly like substances. Wash and drain. Clams are as perishable as fresh fish and should be enjoyed immediately.

    2 quarts coarse-cut raw clams
    1 cup chopped ham
    2 cups chopped onion
    2 cups chopped celery
    1 cup chopped carrots
    2 tablespoons butter
    2 tablespoons flour
    1 quart boiling water
    3 cups diced raw potatoes
    juice of 1/2 lemon
    salt and pepper to taste

Fry ham, onions, celery and carrots in a little oil over low heat until the onions and celery are clear.

Pour off the oil and fat. Add the butter. After it melts, stir in the flour until it is smooth and all has dissolved.

Add the boiling water; let simmer over heat 1 hour.

Add the potatoes and the salt and pepper. When the potatoes are cooked (not over-done so they fall apart) add the lemon juice and the clams. Let cook (simmer to low boil—not a hard boil) 12 minutes.

Serve with crackers.

Freshwater Lobster

The crawfish of freshwater lakes and streams are miniature cousins of the huge saltwater lobsters—and just as tasty.

They may be popped—live—into boiling water. It takes only a few minutes and they are ready to be peeled. Dip the tasty tails in salted, drawn butter.

Displayed whole on a tray they make a great hors d'oeuvres.

chapter VI

PRESERVING MEATS

The first and most important step in preserving game or fish is the care it receives after being shot or caught. Earlier chapters have included detailed suggestions in this regard.

CURING

Our ancestors—before the days of mechanical refrigeration—used salt, and sometimes salt with sugar, as the most common method of preserving meat in warm weather.

Brine Solution - The pork barrel was present in the cellar of most every home and on nearly every farm from colonial times to the early 1900's. Not only pork, but cuts of beef and poultry (including game birds and animals) were preserved in the heavy salt solution. A rule of thumb was to stir in the salt until the solution would float an egg or a potato. This was supposed to indicate that the water had dissolved and absorbed about as much salt as it was going to. (This usually takes about one pound of salt to one gallon of water.) When it was time to use a piece of meat, it was withdrawn from the barrel and allowed to soak overnight in fresh water so that it would not taste too salty. The political expression "pork barrel legislation" comes from the tradition that no matter how long winter wore on, there always seemed to be another piece of meat left in the bottom of the pork barrel; likewise, there always seems to be enough money for the congressmen's pet projects for their home districts.

Dry Salt Treatment - This process simply involves rubbing salt into the meat. If the cuts are less than 3 inches thick, one thorough rubbing should keep the meat from spoiling for several weeks. The meat should be stored, however, in a cool dry room, free from insects, and kept on wood shelving. The cure is considered complete after standing two days for every pound of meat in the cut.

Heavier cuts of meat should be rubbed with salt two or three times at 3 to 5 day intervals.

One pound of salt will usually cure ten pounds of meat. Traditionally, one ounce of saltpeter is added to each 10 pounds of salt to retain an attractive color.

Salt curing is also a treatment used in preparation for smoking.

Salt and Sugar Treatment - Sugar is usually added to salt in the treatment of pork hams. A traditional formula is 8# of salt, 3# of sugar, 3 ounces of saltpeter and 1/2 ounce sodium nitrate. Big game hams (sometimes called rounds or quarters) may be treated the same as pork—but expect a different flavor. A rule of thumb is one ounce of rubbing mixture for each pound of meat.

Rub the ham two or three times at three to five day intervals. The treatment of a large ham takes about a month, storing the meat all that while in a cool, dry, insect free room. Hams may be hung or laid on wood shelving. In the latter case, they should be turned occasionally.

Salt and sugar curing is an excellent preparation for smoking.

Corning - The name usually refers to the process of making corned beef, but other kinds of meat, including wild game, may also be treated in this way. Essentially, the process means submerging meat in a sugar-salt solution under a weight. To avoid corrosion problems, do not use a metal container. Plastic, wood, glass or stone crocks or barrels are all satisfactory.

Prepare the mixture as follows:

    2 gallons water
    4 pounds table or pickling salt
    1 1/2 pounds sugar
    1 teaspoon garlic salt
    1 1/2 ounces sodium nitrate

There should be enough solution from this formula to cover about 50# of meat.

Place a board on top of the meat (preferable cut the shape of the inside of the container) and a heavy clean rock on top of the board.

Let stand for about two weeks or about 3 days per pound of meat.

DRIED BEEF (or round of big game) After the ham has been cured by either the brine or dry treatment, it may be smoked. If the brine cure was used, rinse with cold water and let stand 24 hours before smoking. The length of time required will depend on the temperature and whether you prefer heavy or light smoked flavor. Experience will be your best teacher, but for a start, try forty hours at 130° F. Slice very thin to maximize the flavor. Use for sandwiches or with any chipped beef recipe.

SMOKING - This is probably an even older method of meat preservation than curing. Eskimos and American Indians had been smoking game and fish for unknown generations when the first white men reached this continent. It is used today more for the delicious flavor it imparts to food rather than as a preservative. Smoked fish and game may be kept several weeks in a cool place or under refrigeration. If frozen, it should be kept at a uniform temperature and thawed slowly under refrigeration. It is not safe to keep smoked foods in a warm place or for more than a few weeks. Smoked foods are at their best if enjoyed just after smoking.

Most any wild game or fish may be smoked. Generally speaking, with fish, the more oily species, such as trout, salmon or whitefish—get better results.

Extensive curing is not necessary for game birds or fish. Soaking 24 hours in a brine (heavy salt solution) is adequate.

The length of time required for smoking depends on the heat in the smokehouse. Whereas it takes 30 to 40 hours to smoke game or fish with temperatures just under 100° F., it should require only 15 to 18 hours to do the same job with 130° F. It is not desirable to exceed 140° F. The thickness of meat or fish will also make a difference in the time required.

Individual taste determines whether you want heavy or light smoking. With a little experimenting, you will soon learn how long at which temperature for which kinds of meat, fish and poultry suits you best.

Many varieties of wood are satisfactory, but never use pine, spruce or other resin bearing trees. Hickory, maple, oak or ash are all fine. Fruit woods are also good.

Fish should be gutted, but may be smoked with heads on. It is advisable to leave the skin on; the fish need not be scaled. Large fish will smoke more thoroughly if they are cut in cross sections or are halved (lengthwise along the backbone).

A technique you may like to try with ducks or pheasants is to smoke them head down with a can of vegetable soup in the body cavity. Close off the neck first by twisting a metal tie securely around the neck skin. The soup will help keep the bird moist and will add flavor as well. The soup itself, however, will probably not be to your liking.

A simple smoke house may be constructed from an old icebox or refrigerator by simply placing an electric hot plate in the bottom and heating a pan of hardwood sawdust on the plate.

Here is another easy plan to construct:

Backyard Smoke House

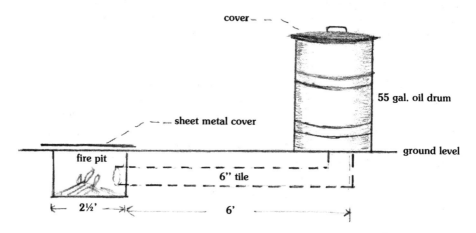

The metal covers over the pit and the barrel may be adjusted to cause a draft, thereby increasing the heat.

CANNING - In this day of the electric freezer, the canning of meat is fast becoming a lost art. Energy shortages could change that. Although canned foods can be kept safely for relatively long periods of time, it is wise to actively boil all canned meats, fish and poultry for a full 15 minutes before eating to remove danger of botulism.

The fastest and safest way to can meat is with the pressure canner. Here are some tips:

- Remove bones after the meat has been cooked.
- For canned poultry and meats
  - use 10# pressure for 75 minutes for pints.
  - use 10# pressure for 90 minutes for quarts

- For canned fish
  - use 10# pressure for 110 minutes for pints
  - do not use quarts.
- If salt is not used in cooking the meat, add 1/2 teaspoon per pint.

FREEZING - There are two keys to preserving quality in frozen meats:

- Keep all air from contacting the meat, and
- Sharp freeze the meat in the coldest spot in the freezer and then keep the temperature in the freezer as constant as possible.

JERKY AND PEMMICAN are time-honored ways of preserving meat, but since the processes used in making these foods are found in Chapter III, they will not be repeated here.

chapter VII

THE WILDERNESS AS YOUR GARDEN

In keeping with the general spirit of this book, this chapter will not concern itself with those things which are edible but not enjoyable. This is not a manual for survival; rather, is a guide for good eating. It is a book designed to help you enjoy the best nature has to offer—taste treats you cannot buy in a supermarket. There are almost countless weeds and plants which may be safely eaten, but not really savored. Even the inner bark of most trees, including the pine, is edible and has some nutritional value if you are facing starvation, but it is hardly enjoyable no matter how we "doctor" it up. Radisson, a founder of the Hudson's Bay Company, recorded in his daily log that when faced with starvation in the cold of winter he even tried making a pudding of the lichens which grow on rocks in the north country. He said it turned black and looked and tasted like glue! We have no hesitation, however, in recommending the following recipes as adventures in good eating.

WILD GREENS

Greens, both wild and domestic, were common table fare in season in most homes across the country in the 1700's and 1800's, and even in the first part of this century. Their preparation is fast becoming a lost art, and this is unfortunate, because we are missing a tasty dish, rich in vitamins.

Some examples well worth trying are dandelions, lambs quarters and even young thistle leaves. It is important that you choose young plants in the spring or early summer.

Salads

Use any of the above mentioned tender greens in place of or in combination with lettuce. Wash the leaves carefully and then chill to crisp. Then create a salad with the traditional ingredients of your choosing.

Greens with Bacon Bits, Sliced Eggs and Mustard Sauce

Clean and wash greens. Boil in salted water until nearly done (wilted); drain.

Meanwhile, hard-boil two eggs.

Cut four slices of lean bacon into bits and fry, but do not let them become burned or hard.

Make a sauce by combining:

    2 eggs
    3 tablespoons vinegar
    1/3 cup milk
    1/2 teaspoon dry mustard
    1 tablespoon sugar
    1 dash salt

Add the greens to the hot skillet containing the bacon bits and bacon grease. Cover with the sauce and stir gently over low heat until the greens are tender.

Garnish with hard-boiled egg slices.

Wild Greens en Casserole

Pick and wash about twice as many greens as it takes to fill the casserole dish you plan to use. Greens will wilt and take up considerably less space when cooked.

Place the greens in a kettle and cover with water. Cook until the greens wilt but remove from heat before the greens lose their color. Drain.

Meanwhile, prepare a white sauce according to your favorite recipe or use this one:

    2 tablespoons butter
    2 tablespoons flour
    1 cup milk
    a little salt and pepper

Melt the butter—carefully, without burning—in a sauce pan or double boiler. Add the flour and continue to cook for three minutes, stirring continuously.

Remove pan from the heat and slowly stir in the cup of milk.

Return the pan to the stove and bring to a boil, stirring all the while.

Place mixture in a double boiler, add salt and pepper, and cook until the sauce thickens.

Beat with an egg beater.

While preparing the sauce, hard-boil three eggs (if they are small, use 4). When cooked, shell and then chop, but not too fine.

Add the eggs to the greens; season lightly with salt and pepper. Gently fold in the white sauce. Transfer the mixture to a buttered casserole dish.

Sprinkle a half-cup of grated cheese over the mixture. Place in a preheated medium oven until the cheese melts. Mushroom pieces or bacon bits could be added to the casserole at the time the sauce is stirred in, for added flavor.

Mock Spinach

Greens, such as dandelions, lambs quarters or young thistle may be prepared as you would spinach by cooking them in a small amount of water (not over-cooked), season lightly and serve with vinegar on the side.

CATTAIL SPROUTS

In early spring, shortly after the snow disappears and the ice melts in the sloughs, cattail sprouts may be found poking up in last year's stands of this marsh weed. Pull them, clean them and prepare them as you would asparagus. Some feel the taste is similar. Later in the year the stems are too woody and tough to use. The sprouts are especially good served with a Hollandaise sauce:

> 3 egg yolks
> 1 1/2 sticks butter or margarine
> 3 tablespoons lemon juice
> 1 dash salt
> 1 pinch cayenne pepper

Warm the butter until soft (not melted). Beat the butter and egg yolks together until creamy. Add the lemon juice and seasonings. Place in a double boiler over boiling water. Stir continuously for three minutes. Remove from heat and stir until the sauce thickens and is smooth.

WOOD FERNS

Collect them in the early spring when they resemble "fiddle necks". Prepare them the same as cattail sprouts (above).

GRAPE LEAVES

Young, tender wild grape leaves may be used in salads or substituted for tame grape leaves in the many Greek and other Mediterranean dishes where meats and/or vegetables are wrapped and then baked in such leaves.

MUSHROOMS

We shall make no attempt here to offer guidance in the picking of mushrooms. The printed page, and even pictures, are no guarantee you will avoid poisonous varieties. We suggest you apprentice yourself to a veteran mushroom picker and learn first-hand.

Morel Mushrooms

Morels need not be peeled. The whole mushroom is edible. Do not soak morels, just brush away any dust or dirt and cut any any defective parts. The lower part of the stalk may be a little tougher and can be removed. The best parts will cut crisp but tender. Slice the mushroom into bite-size pieces and saute in butter until wilted and tender—not browned.

Salt and serve with steaks or chops.

Morels may be canned, frozen or dehydrated.

Puff Ball Mushrooms

Wash the puff balls, but do not soak. Cut away any defective parts.

Slice and dip pieces in your favorite chicken or fish batter. Deep fry.

Small puff balls may be fried whole. Pieces may be added (raw) to stews or gravies during the last few minutes of cooking.

This variety may be canned, frozen or dehydrated.

Shelf Fungus

These range from pale yellow to bright orange in color and are found growing like the shelves they are named for—on trees.

Cut away any defective or woody parts.

Slice into convenient cooking size.

Sauté in butter or deep-fat fry coated with your favorite batter.

Shelf fungus may be canned, but may not be frozen or dehydrated.

Baked Mushrooms

   1 pound thickly sliced mushrooms
   1/2 cup chopped onions
   2 tablespoons lemon juice
   1/2 cup butter
   2 tablespoons flour
   1/3 cup grated cheese
   1/2 cup sour cream
   1/2 cup dry bread crumbs
   salt and pepper

Sauté the mushroom slices with the onions and lemon juice in the butter. When the onions are clear (3 or 4 minutes) season with salt and pepper (lightly) and stir in the flour while still over heat.

Place in a baking dish.

Combine the grated cheese and sour cream and spoon over the mushroom mixture. Sprinkle with bread crumbs and top with a few dabs of butter.

Bake in a hot oven (375 - 400°) for 15 minutes or until a light, golden brown.

Mushroom Stuffing for Fish or Fowl

   3 cups seasoned croutons (or 2 cups cooked wild rice and
      1 cup croutons)
   1 cup chopped celery
   1 cup chopped onion
   1/4 pound butter or margarine
   1 cup sliced mushrooms (need not be precooked,
      but may be)
   salt and pepper
   1/2 cup hot water

Sauté the onions and celery over low heat (in butter) until clear. Add the hot water and pour entire mixture over croutons and/or wild rice. Add mushrooms and season. Stir together. Stuff fowl or fish lightly (do not pack).

Cheese-coated Mushrooms

   2 cups sliced mushrooms
   1 egg beaten into 1 cup of water
   1/2 cup cheese, finely grated
   1/2 cracker crumbs

Mix the cheese and cracker crumbs together. Dip the

mushrooms first into the egg mixture and then roll them in the cracker-cheese combination. Fry in butter or half butter-half olive oil over medium heat until brown.

Creamed Mushrooms

>2 cups mushrooms, sliced (whole if small)
>1 cup cream
>1/4 cup red wine

Sauté the mushrooms in butter. Add the cream and wine and simmer, stirring regularly. You may wish to thicken the sauce with a little flour.

Excellent as a side dish or served over steaks or chops.

Mushroom Side Dish

>1 pound thickly sliced mushrooms
>1/2 stick butter
>1/2 cup chicken or duck broth (or strained chicken soup)
>1/2 teaspoon lemon juice
>   your favorite seasonings or just salt and pepper

Place all ingredients in a covered pan and cook over medium heat for 5 minutes. Remove cover and cook over low heat until nearly all of the liquid has evaporated. Spoon the remaining liquid over the mushrooms and serve.

Broiled Mushrooms

Larger mushrooms or mushroom pieces respond best to this treatment.

Brush first with melted butter and season with a little salt, pepper and nutmeg.

Place under broiler for a few minutes; watch carefully to prevent burning.

Other Uses For Mushrooms

Mushrooms add so much flavor and excitement to hot dishes, casseroles, wild rice dishes and most meats. They can even make a gourmet dish out of a bowl of chili!

chapter VIII

THE WILDERNESS AS YOUR ORCHARD

Wild fruits and berries are usually more flavorful than their cultivated counterparts; however, they tend to be more tart and therefore will require more sugar than traditional recipes. Otherwise, your favorite treatments for sauces, pies, jellies and jams will work very well. Most of the recipes found in this chapter are appropriate for nearly all of the wilderness fruits and berries, including chokecherries, blueberries, raspberries, strawberries, blackberries and June berries.

CHOKECHERRY SYRUP

Great on pancakes, waffles, or French toast or as a topping for ice cream.

    4 cups berries
    2 cups water
    2 cups sugar

Place the above ingredients together in a kettle; bring to a boil, reduce heat so that the liquid will boil slowly until the chokecherries are soft. Force the mixture through a sieve. Stir in sugar and return to stove; let simmer, stirring constantly until it thickens. Remember the thickening will increase as the mixture cools. Pour into sterilized glass jars and seal. If the syrup will be kept under refrigeration or in a cool place, an ordinary screw cap such as found on a mayonnaise jar will suffice.

This recipe also works well with most other berries but in the case of blueberries or strawberries, for example, you may prefer not to strain out the pulp.

CHOKECHERRY AND WINE JELLY

1 cup Chokecherry juice (or use 2 cups of chokecherry syrup and omit the sugar)
1 cup red wine
3 cups sugar
1/2 bottle liquid pectin

To make juice, cover the berries with water, bring to a boil and then let simmer until the berries soften. Force through a sieve or jelly bag.

Mix the juice, wine and sugar in a kettle until the sugar dissolves.

Bring to a boil as you stir; let boil 1 minute (continue stirring).

Remove from the stove and gradually stir in the pectin. Ladle into preheated jars or jelly glasses.

Seal (paraffin will do).

BLUEBERRY JELLY

2 cups juice (Make juice by following procedure explained above for chokecherries)
4 cups sugar
1 teaspoon lemon juice (or whatever citrus juice you have handy)
1 bottle fruit pectin

Stir the juice, sugar and lemon juice together until the sugar dissolves. Bring to a boil. Add a restaurant size pat of butter to reduce foaming. Stir constantly. After the mixture comes to a full boil, remove from heat and add pectin. Return to the stove and let boil 1 minute, stirring all the while. Skim off any foam. Ladle into heated sterilized jelly glasses and seal with paraffin.

BLUEBERRY JAM

4 cups cleaned blueberries
5 cups sugar
1 cup water

Mix together all of the above ingredients. Bring to a boil and then reduce heat so that it will boil slowly, for 15 minutes or until thick. Stir all the while, crushing the berries occasionally with a spoon. If the mixture is too dry at any point to boil freely, add a little water.

Ladle into sterilized glasses or jars and seal.

BLUEBERRY SAUCE

Most any wild berries may be used with this updated version of an old favorite recipe.

    4 cups berries (carefully picked over and cleaned)
    2/3 cup sugar
    3 tablespoons corn starch (flour may be substituted)
    2 cups water (hot)
    2 tablespoons lemon or other citrus juice
    1/2 teaspoon salt
    2 pats butter

Combine the sugar, cornstarch and salt.

Add the lemon juice to the hot water. Stir this mixture, a little at a time, into the dry mixture. When it is smooth, place over low heat and cook until it thickens, stirring occasionally.

Add blueberries and continue simmering until the sauce has the desired "thickness", remembering that it will thicken still more as it cools.

Remove from the stove and stir in the butter as it melts.

This also makes an excellent syrup; just continue the heating and stirring process until it is "syrupy".

WILD CRANBERRIES

Minnesota, Wisconsin, Michigan, New England and Ontario have hundreds of wild cranberry bogs hidden away in tamarack and spruce swamps. Finding them is a real challenge, and don't count on anyone showing you their favorite spot! The cranberries are often hidden under the foliage and often defy detection. Oh yes, you'll need a pair of hip boots!

Once you find the cranberries, you may cook them with the very same recipes you use for those purchased in the supermarket. Here are a few that may be new to you, however:

Cranberry Relish

Wash the berries and let dry.

Put them through a grinder or chopper, making a cranberry pulp.

For each cup of pulp add 1 cup of sugar. Stir until the sugar is completely blended into the pulp.

For a more tart flavor, add 2 tablespoons lemon or orange juice for each cup of pulp.

Serve with any wild game, but what could be better than wild cranberries with wild turkey or duck?

CRANBERRY STUFFING

Use your favorite stuffing recipe but add one cup chopped, raw wild cranberries.

WILD CRANBERRY TEA

Prepare the juice by mixing together in a kettle:

    4 cups cranberries
    2 cups sugar
    2 cups water

Boil until the cranberries are soft; stir while the mixture boils. Force the juice out of the mixture through a sieve or jelly bag.
To 2 quarts of juice, add:

    2 cinnamon sticks
    juice of 1 lemon
    juice of two oranges
    2 cups of sugar (more or less according to taste)

Simmer the cranberry juice with the cinnamon sticks for 5 minutet. Remove from stove and stir in sugar until it dissolves. Add citrus juices. Stir until mixture is thoroughly blended. Keep refrigerated and covered.
Heat to serve.

HIGH BUSH CRANBERRY JELLY

These grow on large bushes and are not true cranberries. They will not work well with any of the low bush recipes, but they do make an excellent, tangy, bright red jelly. They will make a dreadful smell in your kitchen, but the product is well worth the inconvenience.
To render the juice, add 3 cups of water to 2 cups of berries. Let simmer 5 minutes; mashing the fruit as it cooks. Strain out the juice through a sieve or jelly bag.
Add 2/3 cup of sugar to each cup of juice.
Bring to a boil and then let simmer 15 minutes, stirring all the while.
Remove from heat, add 1 bottle fruit pectin.
Return to heat and let boil 1 minute, stirring continuously.
Skim off foam and ladle into preheated glasses. Seal. (Paraffin will do.)

ROSE HIPS

This favorite and versatile wilderness fruit is an excellent source of vitamin C. The hips may be collected after the first frost when they are a bright red. Wash them and remove the brushes.

Juice

Cover the cleaned hips with water and let simmer 15 minutes (or a little longer, if they are especially large hips). When the fruit is soft, squash gently with a spoon. Strain the juice through a jelly bag or sieve.

Tea

The juice may be served hot as a tea. If it is too strong, add hot water. If you prefer sweet drinks, add sugar to taste. For a spicy drink, add 2 cinnamon sticks and let simmer 5 minutes.

Jelly

    2 cups rose hip juice
    4 cups sugar
    1 tablespoon lemon juice
    1/2 bottle fruit pectin

Mix the first three ingredients together in a kettle and stir until the sugar dissolves. Bring solution to a slow boil and then boil hard 1 minute, stirring constantly. Add 1/2 bottle fruit pectin and boil an additional minute. Skim off any foam and ladle into preheated sterilized jars or jelly glasses. Seal.

Syrup

Follow the jelly recipe but do not add pectin. Let simmer, stirring regularly, until the liquid thickens; remember it will become more syrupy as it cools.

Store refrigerated or seal in jars.

Jam

    8 cups cleaned hips (brushes removed as well)
    4 cups water

Boil, covered, 20 minutes. Process the cooked hips through a food mill or sieve to form a puree.

Slice 1 lemon very thin and cut each slice into several wedges or pie shapes. Cook the lemon for a few minutes in a little water.

To 4 cups of puree, add the lemon juice, lemon pulp and 1 1/2 pound sugar.

Cook, slowly, until quite thick and clear.

Ladle into sterilized glasses and seal with paraffin.

WILD ROSE PETAL CUPCAKES

Collect enough rose petals so that when torn into small pieces they will fill one cup (not pressed down).

Using your favorite recipe for a dozen cupcakes, add the petals (torn into small pieces) at the same time you add the flour. Mix the petals uniformly into the batter.

Unlike most recipes in this book, you can't save any money on this one, but it will give you a good excuse to get out of doors on a beautiful day in early June!

WILD GRAPE JELLY

Wild grapes are more tart but not as flavorful as the big, blue concords. Wild grape jelly, however, goes just great with wild duck or a venison roast—and it isn't bad on toast either! Some prefer to use 1/2 tame grapes and thereby add their rich flavor to the light, tartness of the wild variety.

Extract the juice by adding enough water to cover the grapes in a kettle. Crush the grapes and bring to a boil. Let simmer, covered, about 10 minutes. Pour into a jelly bag and squeeze out the juice.

> 5 cups juice
> 7 cups sugar

Stir the sugar into the juice until it dissolves. Return to stove and again bring to a boil, stirring all the while.

Add 1/2 bottle fruit pectin and boil hard 1 minute.

Remove from heat and add a pat of butter to reduce foam. Skim off any foam that does form and ladle into sterilized glasses or jars and seal (paraffin).

WILD GRAPE NECTAR

A concentrate which takes up less storage space and can be made into a beverage by diluting it with cold water can be created by using the same procedure just described above for making jelly, but do not add the pectin. Instead, continue boiling and stirring until it has a syrupy consistency.

The syrup may also be used as an ice cream topping or as a flavoring agent.

Do not expect wild grape products to taste like domestic varieties.

WILD GRAPE JUICE

You may use the process described in extracting juice to make the grape jelly, or try this method:

2 cups wild grapes
1 cup sugar

Wash the grapes. Use only the ripe ones. Remove all stems. Place the grapes in a quart jar (preheated). Add sugar and fill with boiling water to within 1/4 inch of the top of the jar. Cap and place in hot water bath for 10 minutes.

SYRUPY WILD STRAWBERRY SAUCE

This is especially good on shortcake, pancakes, waffles or ice cream. Wild strawberries are very small, but extremely flavorful and well worth the effort to pick.

2 cups cleaned berries
1 teaspoon vinegar
enough water to cover berries
1 1/2 cups sugar

Cover the strawberries with water, add the vinegar, and boil for 1 minute. Stir in the sugar (thoroughly) and simmer 15 minutes.

Use fresh or preserve in sealed jars. It will keep several days under refrigeration, however.

Regular sauce may be made by using the same procedure, but do not simmer more than a few minutes.

WILD BLACKBERRY (SOMETIMES CALLED DEWBERRY) JAM

4 cups blackberries
6 cups sugar
1 orange—ground or chopped
1 lemon—ground or chopped
1 cup water
a dash of baking soda (fraction teaspoon)
1 bottle fruit pectin

Combine the chopped lemon and orange with the soda and water. Simmer for 20 minutes. Do not let it dry out; in that case add a little more water.

Add berries and sugar. Stir together. Add enough water so that the mixture can boil freely. Bring to a boil and then reduce heat and let simmer 10 minutes.

Remove from heat and stir in the pectin.

Skim off foam and ladle into hot jars or jelly glasses.

PINCHERRY JELLY

Extract the juice by adding 3 cups of water to 2 cups of berries. Simmer about 5 minutes as you mash the berries. Strain through a jelly bag or sieve.

Return the juice to the stove and bring to a boil. Then lower the temperature and let simmer 15 minutes, stirring regularly.

Remove from heat and add 1 bottle fruit pectin. Skim off foam and ladle into hot jelly glasses. Seal with paraffin.

The jelly will be clear and a very bright red.

A cup of red wine added during the last 15 minutes of simmering will give the jelly an exciting taste.

SPICY JAMS AND JELLIES

Add 1/2 teaspoon each of:
>   ground cloves
>   ground allspice
>   ground cinnamon

before the final boiling or simmering process starts. The spicy taste goes especially well with blueberry, blackberry and rose hip jellies.

MIXED FRUIT JELLIES

The juices of some berries and fruits may be combined to attain special textures and flavors. For example, apple juice may be added to chokecherries, wild plums, rose hips or wild grapes. Don't be afraid to experiment.

A combination that will have your family and guests guessing is to use equal parts of most any berry juice and sumac juice. To extract sumac juice, cover the red berries with water and boil a few minutes and then strain.

Sumac has been called the "lemonade of the wilderness".

WILD PLUM BUTTER

Wash and remove blemished or spoiled areas.

Make plum pulp by covering the fruit with water (just barely) and then boil until the plums are soft. Force through a sieve or food mill.

To each cup of pulp, add 2/3 cup of sugar. Cook until thick, stirring regularly. It should take about a half-hour.

Ladle into preheated glasses and seal.

For a little spicier flavor, add a tablespoon of cinnamon and a tablespoon of cloves to each cup of pulp before cooking.

LABRADOR TEA

Use the narrow green leaves (usually an orangish brown on the underside) of this plant found on tundra and muskeg. Dry the leaves before use. Use about a cup of leaves to 8 cups of boiling water. Let boil for about 10 minutes.

This nutritious tea has been used by frontiersmen for generations.

CATTAIL PANCAKES

Very honestly, the chief virtue of this recipe is more in conversation than in flavor—but it won't spoil the pancakes!

Just add 1/2 cup cattail fluff to 1 1/2 cups of flour as you prepare your favorite pancake recipe. The fluff is more easily harvested in the fall.

FRUIT LEATHER

Fruit leather is an interesting, different, but delicious way of preserving and using wild fruits and berries. The "leather" may be used as a snack and is especially appropriate as a convenient nourishment during out of doors activities. It may also be chopped into tiny pieces as a colorful flavoring ingredient for use in cookies, holiday breads and cakes. It can even serve to flavor beverages.

To make fruit leather, use most any wild fruit or berries or a combination thereof. After cleaning, blend into a puree. If the fruit has stones or large seeds (such as wild plums or chokecherries) remove these first. If the fruit is large, cut into small pieces. The simplest and fastest way to make the puree is in a blender.

Add two tablespoons of honey or sugar to each cup of puree (use more or less according to your taste).

Add 1 teaspoon of lemon juice to each cup of puree to prevent discoloration.

For special flavor treatment, stir in any of the following: (The amount of each and the combinations are up to you. Much of the fun of making fruit leather comes from experimenting.) Cinnamon, nutmeg, raisins, coconut, nuts, grated citrus fruit peel, or your favorite granola ingredients.

Line a flat, shallow pan with "Saran Wrap" or a similar plastic. If necessary, use tape to hold it in place.

Pour a thin layer of puree into the pan, covering all areas but keeping the mixture no more than 1/4 inch deep.

Place in a very low oven (140°). Let dry until the surface is no longer sticky to the touch.

Remove from heat; remove plastic; and return sheet of fruit to the pan to cool (out of the oven).

Roll into cylindrical shapes and wrap in plastic or foil. Store in a cool, dry, dark place.

NUTS

Filberts, hazel nuts and butternuts all grow wild in the Upper Midwest and Ontario. They are ready for picking in August or early fall when the shells are well formed, hard and can be removed from the protecting foliage. The nuts may be removed far easier, however, if the husks are dried first by placing them on a garage or shed roof, in a single layer, where the sun can dry them until the nuts almost fall out. Nuts may also be dried by packing them, loosely, in the inside part of a minnow bucket and then hanging the bucket from a tree limb.

Nuts are best stored in their shells—but examine each for worm holes and discard those so infected or the worms will move from nut to nut! A covered, gallon plastic or glass jar makes an excellent container for storage.

Wild, cracked nuts make a great fireside snack on a winter night or may be used in homemade cookies, candy, breads and cakes or may be crushed for use as a dessert topping.

Acorns may also be eaten, but they are not as tasty, frankly, as the nuts just described! But if you are interested in something a little different, shell the acorns, let them soak in water overnight; and then roast them in a slow oven until they are nut-hard. Season with salt or glaze them with a mixture of milk and sugar. They may also be chopped for use in baking.

Certain Indian tribes made a flour from the acorns and used them in making a type of bread.

chapter IX

TURTLES AND FROGS

Ugly—but good eating!

The snapping turtle is the only one of its species considered good to eat on this part of the continent. Yet, in the world of turtles, it is probably the least beautiful and most ill-tempered.

BUTCHERING TURTLES

Both the claws and the head are "lethal", and should be removed before operating. Begin by chopping off the head. Let the turtle hang, head down for a couple of hours because the nervous system will react at least that long after the head is removed. The "dying" process can be speeded up by boiling the turtle for a half hour; this will also make it easier to clean. Now chop off the claws. The first few times you try it the turtle will be easier to handle if you lay him on his back on a board or old table and drive a nail through each "claw".

The next step is to remove the bottom shell. Locate the soft cartilage "crack" where the upper and lower shells are joined on each side; this may be cut with a knife. Cut away any skin that holds the lower shell. After removing the lower shell, skin the legs and remove them - including the thighs. Next, remove the meat around the neck and at the base of the shell (tail end). You will have now salvaged about 90% of the meat, so the re-mainder may be discarded.

TURTLE SOUP
(Or use less water and call it stew)

Turtle meat is usually tough. Allow enough cooking time to tenderize it.

For about 2 pounds of turtle meat—cut bite size—you will need the following ingredients:

    1/2 cup flour
    cooking oil
    seasoning (salt, pepper and your favorite soup or stew
        seasoning—such as beau monde)
    1 large onion, chopped
    other vegetables of your choosing, such as:
    1 cup celery, cut into ½ to 1 inch pieces
    4 medium potatoes, cut bite size
    1 large can tomatos
    4 large carrots, sliced thick
    1 medium rutabaga, cut bite size
    2 cubes beef or chicken bouillon[1]—or use soup starter
        according to the recipe on the package for 2 quarts
        of water.

Season the cut up meat with salt and pepper, roll in flour and brown in a heavy skillet over medium heat (in cooking oil).

Place the browned turtle in a kettle or crock pot, cover with 2 quarts[2] of water. Let simmer for one hour. After the first 30 minutes, add the chopped onion, bouillon cubes and any other seasonings you like in soup or stew.

After the hour, add the vegetables and let simmer for a second hour or until the vegetables are well done.

TURTLE GUMBO

For 2 to 3 pounds of bite-size turtle meat, you will need the following ingredients:

    ½ cup flour
    cooking oil and 1 stick butter or margarine
    1 can mushroom pieces
    1 clove garlic, diced very fine
    1 green pepper, chopped
    1 medium onion, chopped
    1 cup celery, chopped
    1 #2 can tomato sauce or 1 small can tomato puree
    ½ cup cooking wine (red)
    seasoning—salt and pepper plus 2 drops Tabasco sauce

Lightly season the turtle meat with salt and pepper and dredge in flour. Fry in cooking oil and margarine (or butter). Use a heavy skillet and medium heat.

[1]Either beef or chicken bouillon is appropriate because parts of the turtle taste a little like chicken and other parts taste more like beef or veal.
[2]The amount of water really depends on how thick you like your soup or stew. More can always be added at the time you add the vegetables if you are in doubt.

When the meat is browned, add all other ingredients plus enough water to just barely cover the meat. Let simmer for 1 hour and serve over a bed of rice or boiled potatoes. You may have to add a little water during the hour of simmering to prevent dryness, but a fairly thick sauce is desirable.

BATTERED TURTLE

Snapping turtle is rarely tender enough to fry; therefore, it is a good idea to parboil the pieces first. This is done by letting the meat simmer in seasoned water[3] for about 30 - 40 minutes.

Deep fry turtle as you would chicken, using your favorite batter. A simple batter recipe you might like to try calls for complete-mix pancake flour (the kind where you just add water). Do not make the batter too heavy or it will insulate the turtle meat. For added flavor, use ½ cooking wine and ½ water to make the batter. If you like it "crunchy" add a cup of finely-broken corn flakes.

BAKED TURTLE

Place serving size pieces of turtle in a kettle or crock-pot and cover with water.

Add the following:

        1 large onion, chopped
        1 cup celery, chopped
        2 teaspoons salt
        8 peppercorns
        2 bay leaves

Let simmer for a full hour.

Transfer the meat to a greased roaster, laying the pieces in a single layer. Use a slotted spoon to strain out the onions and celery and sprinkle over the pieces of meat. Mushroom slices may also be added if you wish. Place a generous pat of butter on each piece of meat.

Cover and bake in a medium oven (300-325°) for 1 to 1½ hours or until tender. For added flavor, place a custard dish of red cooking wine in a corner of the roaster during the baking process.

BUTCHERING FROGS

The so-called bull frog is the only variety of frog worth the effort of cleaning and preparing. The ordinary bait frog is edible

[3]Salt and pepper or other favorite spices.

but there is so little meat on the toothpick size drum sticks they just aren't worth the effort—unless, of course, you are facing starvation or are looking for a novel hors d'oeuvres that is sure to stimulate conversation. Do not use tree frogs or toads!

Cleaning is not difficult. Amputate the leg at the hip. Cut off the feet. Remove the skin as you would take off a glove.

FRIED FROG LEGS

This is the simplest and best treatment. Use any kind of oil or shortening, but a combination of cooking oil and butter or butter alone seems to give the best flavor. If you use butter, keep the heat low so as not to burn the legs. Dredge in seasoned flour or roll in cracker crumbs. If the legs are large, you may want to use an egg and water batter to dip them in before rolling them in cracker or bread crumbs and then deep fry them.

Frog legs get done quickly, even over low heat, but be sure they are done! The meat should separate easily from the bone when they are ready to serve. Because the legs vary so much in size it is difficult to specify an exact time, but they shouldn't take more than ten minutes. Turn the legs, of course, so as to cook them uniformly and prevent burning.